T0285139

.

EQUALITY OF OPPORTUNITY

A CENTURY OF DEBATE

EQUALITY OF OPPORTUNITY

DAVID DAVENPORT
GORDON LLOYD

HOOVER INSTITUTION PRESS
Stanford University | Stanford, California

hoover.org

Hoover Institution Press Publication No. 732
Hoover Institution at Leland Stanford Junior University,
Stanford, California 94305-6003

First printing 2023
29   28   27   26   25   24   23   7   6   5   4   3   2   1

Manufactured in the United States of America
Printed on acid-free, archival-quality paper

Library of Congress Cataloging-in-Publication Data
Names: Davenport, David, 1950– author. | Lloyd, Gordon, 1942– author.
Title: Equality of opportunity : a century of debate / David Davenport and
   Gordon Lloyd.
Other titles: Hoover Institution Press publication ; 732.
Description: Stanford, California : Hoover Institution Press, Stanford
   University, 2023. | Series: Hoover Institution Press publication ; no.
   732 | Includes bibliographical references and index. | Summary:
   "Considers the differing views of equality of opportunity in the United
   States—from the Founders' conception to that of political
   progressives—and the role of the government in advancing it"—Provided
   by publisher.
Identifiers: LCCN 2022059586 (print) | LCCN 2022059587 (ebook) | ISBN
   9780817925840 (cloth) | ISBN 9780817925864 (epub) | ISBN 9780817925888
   (pdf)
Subjects: LCSH: Equality—United States—History. | Opportunity—United
   States—History. | United States—Social policy. | United
   States—Economic policy.
Classification: LCC HN90.S6 D377 2023 (print) | LCC HN90.S6 (ebook) | DDC
   305.0973—dc23/eng/20230206
LC record available at https://lccn.loc.gov/2022059586
LC ebook record available at https://lccn.loc.gov/2022059587

CONTENTS

INTRODUCTION

This is now our fourth, and doubtless final, short book exploring how the Franklin Roosevelt and Herbert Hoover debates of the 1930s became the paradigm for debates today between liberals and conservatives. Although Roosevelt and Hoover did not debate directly and in person, their speeches and writings laid out a classic conflict between those who, like Hoover, believe the American system created by the Founders is still the best hope for America and those who, like Roosevelt, feel the American system needs a radical transformation.

This book is like our earlier title, *Rugged Individualism: Dead or Alive?*, in which we took up a classic American philosophical doctrine and asked what has happened to it over the years. In the case of rugged individualism, a term coined by Herbert Hoover in his 1928 presidential campaign, the doctrine has been questioned and attacked, but has somehow survived in the hearts and minds of Americans such that political efforts to overturn or radically transform it have so far not succeeded.

Similarly, we ask what has happened to equality of opportunity, a term that came to the fore in the Hoover-Roosevelt era. Hoover described and defended the American system as one based on rugged individualism coupled with equality of opportunity. On the other hand, Roosevelt, in his famous

Commonwealth Club speech in 1932, said "equality of opportunity as we have known it no longer exists." The doctrine has had its ups and downs, its defenders and attackers, over the years, but it is still alive and an important part of the conversation today.

Little did we know that, when we started this book, the social justice movements of the early 2020s would bring equality questions, including equality of opportunity, to the forefront of seemingly everything from political debates to business endorsements and the arts. We should acknowledge, then, that this is not a book about social justice in the 2020s. Nor do we seek to address all the social, economic, employment, educational, and legal questions raised by current debates.

While some of these current issues are reflected in chapter 5—summarizing the progressive vs. conservative debates over equality of opportunity today—the purpose of this book is to locate, as we did in *Rugged Individualism*, an important American doctrine implicit in the Founding and brought to light by the Herbert Hoover–Franklin Roosevelt debates of the 1930s. We then follow the equality of opportunity debate through three of our most consequential presidencies: Franklin Roosevelt and his New Deal, Lyndon Johnson and his Great Society, and Ronald Reagan and his counterrevolution. We seek to ask and pose answers to the question: Whatever happened to equality of opportunity?

In all our work, we seek to "go back to come back." That is, we feel that by looking to history, we can gain important insight into the policy debates of the day. We are hopeful that this effort will make such a contribution for equality of opportunity.

CHAPTER ONE

The Origins of Equality of Opportunity

For at least one hundred years and still counting, Americans have debated what equality of opportunity means. To some, it is closely tied to freedom, centering on the right of each individual to pursue whatever life or calling he or she may choose. To others, it is more a question of circumstances and the limits those may place on one's ability to make life choices. Are all Americans born with equality of opportunity and, therefore, free to choose their own path? Or is equality of opportunity something that must be created by evening out inequalities innate in each person's abilities as well as those defined by their economic and social circumstances?

Soon this debate turns to the role of government in equality of opportunity. If equality of opportunity is primarily a question of legal and political rights, the government's role would involve setting forth and defending individual rights and the freedom to choose. If, on the other hand, equality of opportunity is about a level playing field, the government's responsibility would expand to include education and policies designed to achieve economic and social equality. The former implies a more limited role for government, essentially leaving the individual free to pursue his or her own opportunities. The latter brings the government directly onto the playing field, passing laws and enacting policies in an attempt to create greater equality and opportunity.

In order to understand this very current and lively debate, we must turn back to the time when each view came onto the scene. First, we should revisit the Founding era of our nation and the drafting of the Declaration of Independence and the Constitution, when equality of opportunity was understood as a question of securing rights through limited government. It was then, according to the Founders, up to each individual to pursue "Life, Liberty and the pursuit of Happiness."

Then we must travel from the late 1700s of the Founding era to the early 1900s of the Progressive era. The Progressives argued that the limited role of government advocated by the Founders had left in place vast inequalities in living conditions. They argued that government should be far more active in providing a fair deal, or what President Franklin D. Roosevelt would call a "New Deal" for "the forgotten man." In the Progressive view, it was both necessary and proper for government to undertake the responsibility of creating equality of opportunity through governmental social and economic policies.

Focusing this debate narrowly on equality of opportunity is a challenge, because this was not a term the Founders used. In fact, the Founders felt that equality, broadly speaking, was something Americans already had as a natural right, and the government's role was to defend and protect it. The Progressives, on the other hand, called out equality of opportunity specifically as something that had been lost. For the Founders, then, equality was something you moved *from* and for the Progressives, it was something to move *toward*. Even with these differences, however, reconstructing the debate over equality of opportunity proves to be a useful and important exercise.

This is still a debate today. Is equality of opportunity something for each individual to pursue as best he or she can, under a limited government? Or is equality of opportunity something the government itself can and should seek to create? We propose to join this debate by imagining the Founders, and especially James Madison, the father of the Constitution, arguing the case against the Progressives, particularly Woodrow Wilson, one of our first progressive presidents. This Founders-Progressives debate effectively sets the stage for understanding the differing views about equality of opportunity today.

Madison, The Founders, and Equality of Opportunity

Noted British astronomer and mathematician Fred Hoyle expressed the importance of history in understanding the present when he said, "Things are the way they are because they were the way they were." In order to comprehend the nature of the equality that Madison and his fellow Founders wanted to pursue in the new world, we must begin by understanding the nature of the *inequality* of opportunity that existed in the Old World they left behind. Indeed, since equality of opportunity per se was not extensively debated by the Founders and the Progressives, we must look for strong clues about it in two places: the inequality each sought to overcome and the form of government each saw as likely to create appropriate equality.

For all of its advanced thinking about governance, the Britain that was home to the Founding generation was socially and politically a class system. One was born into a certain position in life, perhaps a monarch or aristocrat, more likely a worker or a serf, with very little mobility among the groups. These practices were extended to Britain's colonies as well, leaving the American colonies vulnerable to this sort of continuation of European inequality. Monarchy and aristocracy should not, the founders agreed, have any place in the New World. Indeed, when understanding the nature of the equality of opportunity that the founders sought to create, the rejection of monarchy and class were at the heart of the matter.

Therefore, it was vital that the Declaration of Independence state, in its second paragraph, the "self-evident" truth that "all men are created equal." Further, the Declaration continued, all are "endowed by their Creator with certain unalienable Rights, that among these are Life, Liberty and the pursuit of Happiness." Clearly in the New World, the old notions that people were born by nature to be inevitably an aristocrat or a peasant, a monarch or a subject, would not be part of the new order of things. Rather, people were created equal and had the unalienable right to pursue happiness each in their own way. Put differently, human beings not only had an inherent ability to govern themselves but they had the right, by "the Laws of Nature," to do so.

With citizens possessing the liberty to pursue equality of opportunity, the question then arises: What form of government would best assure the equality of opportunity claimed by the Declaration of Independence? It is on this question, especially, that the thinking of James Madison would come to the fore. For Madison and his fellow Founders, the government that would best protect both liberty and equality was a republican form, one that not would allow any place for monarchy or aristocracy. As Benjamin Franklin put it in response to the question of what kind of government the Founders had established: "A republic, if you can keep it."

By the eighteenth century, republicanism was embraced as the preferred alternative to monarchy, or rule by one for private benefit; aristocracy, or rule by the few who are better than the rest of us; and democracy, or direct rule of the many. The republican form of government had been tested successfully at the state level prior to the adoption of the national constitution. All appealed to "the people" as the only legitimate source of authority. Common features were representative government with regular elections, no titles of nobility or primogeniture, fewer restraints on who could vote and run for office, and protection of freedom of the press and liberty of conscience. Even though the Declaration of Independence had left open the particular form of government to be chosen, each state selected a democratic republican form to secure the twin goals of liberty and equality.[1]

While the states were rapidly embracing the republican form of government, the limited Articles of Confederation prevailed at the continental level. Between 1781 and 1787, leaders such as James Madison, Alexander Hamilton, and George Washington argued that something had gone wrong with the American experiment in self-government. They saw the principles of the American Revolution at risk because state legislatures were dominant and the majority were passing laws that undermined both the liberty of individuals and the public good. Each state had the power and equal opportunity to go its own way, and the federal government under the Articles had only the limited powers that were explicitly expressed. There was no federal champion capable of guarding liberty and equality.

A desire to avoid the old European inequalities of class, monarchy, and aristocracy was very much part of the debates leading to the adoption of the US Constitution. The Antifederalists, who opposed ratification of the Constitution, were concerned that it held the potential for the president to become a monarch, or for the senate or judiciary to become an aristocracy. Therefore, Article I, Section 9 of the Constitution expressly states that "No Title of Nobility shall be granted by the United States," and the acceptance of a "Title, of any kind whatever, from any King, Prince, or foreign State" required "the Consent of the Congress." Rather than monarchs or aristocrats making the rules, Madison and the Founders sought representatives elected by the people who, working within several filters and systems of the Constitution, would deliberate over what the government should do. The "people's House" of Representatives, as it is called, would promote equality of political opportunity over and against aristocracy and monarchy.

Madison then focused on the American challenge that is still with us today: how to protect both liberty and equality. He saw the question as how to protect majority rule, that is to say equality, as well as minority rights, or liberty. The assumption was that the rights of the majority are protected by the principle of majority rule. The challenge, then, of the republican form is to protect the liberty and rights of the minority also. In a sense this is a fundamental dilemma of American political life: Can we have both majority rule and minority rights? Or: Can we have equality and liberty too?

Madison took up these questions in Federalist No. 10, the most famous of the Federalist Papers. He argued that part of the reconciliation between equality and liberty requires an understanding of human nature, which—unlike the later Progressives—he thought was fixed and not malleable. Human beings are quarrelsome and contentious by nature—or, as Madison famously put it, faction is "sown in the nature of man." Madison added that "the most common and durable form of faction has been the various and unequal distribution of property. Those who hold, and those who are without property, have ever formed distinct interests in society." To pursue equality to its fullest form, to quote Madison in Federalist No. 10, would mean giving "to every citizen the same opinions, passions, and interests," something both unrealistic and, with individual liberty, undesirable.[2] Alexander Hamilton agreed with Madison: "The door" to advancement in society "ought to be equally open to all." But human nature informs us that "there are strong minds in every walk of life, that will rise superior to the disadvantages of the situation, and will commend the tribute due to their merit."[3] Noah Webster, in 1788, similarly encouraged the idea of equal opportunity for all as "essential to the continuance of republican government" through "a system of education as gives every citizen an opportunity of acquiring knowledge and fitting himself for places of trust."[4]

Government alone will not be able to deal with "these clashing interests" since, as Madison pointed out in Federalist No. 10, "enlightened statesmen will not always be at the helm." A pure democracy would not be a helpful solution since the majority could overrun the rights of the minority in the heat of the moment. Indeed, Madison most feared what he called a majority faction. What is needed instead, Madison continued in Federalist No. 10, is a republican form of government in which points of view are filtered through the electoral process and the deliberation of elected representatives. Madison then advanced the new idea that this process of refining and enlarging the public views could be better achieved not in a small republic but rather in a large one, where more good officials are available for election and where it would be more difficult to inflame the entire country with particular passions. In this kind of large republic, ambition would counteract ambition, allowing greater protection of both majority and minority rights.

The formula by which equality would be achieved for Madison and the Founders was through these two powerful ideas: liberty as the philosophical base, and the republican form of government as the system to protect it. Liberty affords each individual the right to make his or her own choices, unconstrained by any political power such as a monarchy or aristocracy. A republic provides the opportunity both for majority rights, or equality, and for minority rights, or liberty. Thomas Jefferson described this combination, in his first inaugural address, as a "sacred principle," that "the will of the majority is in all cases to prevail" but the minority possesses "their equal rights which equal law must protect." Or, as Madison succinctly put it: "equal laws protecting equal rights."[5] Equality, liberty, and the republican form: these three summarize the Madisonian approach of the Founders.

All this came together and worked well in the New World. Immigrants flocked to America, then as now, because they saw it as a land of opportunity. Founder Benjamin Franklin described some of the opportunities Europeans might find there, noting in particular the availability of land, which was not occupied and could be obtained cheaply, allowing farmers to own land and build businesses they could never undertake in Europe. Franklin pointed out the greater possibilities for one's children to grow up into fine careers away from the crowded professions of Europe. Notably, he felt the greater opportunity in America led to greater equality as well, with fewer rich and poor but instead "a general happy Mediocrity that prevails."[6]

The French historian J. Hector St. John de Crèvecoeur, who himself relocated to the New World, also wrote about the differences between life in Europe and America in a 1782 essay.[7] He noted the relative equality in America, with "rich and poor not so far removed from each other as they are in Europe." He admired the "pleasing uniformity of decent competence" found in American habitations, contrasted with the castles and hovels to be found in Europe. "Here man is free as he ought to be," he said, "nor is this pleasing equality so transitory as many others are." The American is a new man, Crèvecoeur concluded, delivered "from involuntary idleness, service dependence, penury, and useless labour" to "toils of a very different nature, rewarded by ample subsistence."

The French journalist and philosopher Alexis de Tocqueville would later comment on the spirit of liberty and equality he observed when he toured America and penned his *Democracy in America* (1835). Tocqueville was surprised by the extent of equality in the new country, saying, "No novelty struck me more vividly during my stay there than the equality of conditions." Americans were born equal, rather than having to become equal. He included the ready availability of land as a factor in creating equality, noting that the very "soil of America" was "opposed to territorial aristocracy." This is undergirded by its constitution, creating a nation of equal citizens. But it was also part of the culture of the New World since, as he wrote, "The democratic people's . . . passion for equality is ardent, insatiable, eternal and invincible." And to combat the dangers associated with "equality of conditions," the only true remedy is "political freedom."[8]

At the time of the Founding, one must concede, this equality was largely limited to white males, and the extension of equality to women and people of color would arrive later. But Founders are not closers; they lay the foundations for themselves and their posterity. It was left to Abraham Lincoln and the Civil War to extend individual liberty and equality of opportunity to former slaves. The Nineteenth Amendment to the Constitution in 1920 followed the spirit of the "Remember the Ladies" letter of 1776 from Abigail Adams to John Adams, extending voting rights to women.[9] There was now a federal champion capable of guarding personal liberty and equality.

Abraham Lincoln: The Civil War and Constitutional Bridge

One cannot travel the equality of opportunity road from the Founders of the late eighteenth century to the Progressives of the early twentieth century without passing over an essential bridge: Abraham Lincoln, the Civil War, and the Civil War amendments to the Constitution. Lincoln and the Civil War provide important transitional, indeed transformative, components to the debate between Madison and Wilson about equality of opportunity. Fundamentally, several aspects of equality of opportunity became federal matters, with new rights established by constitutional amendment. This bridge to greater federal guarantees of equality also opened the door to a larger role for the federal government debated during the Progressive era and beyond.

The Thirteenth Amendment (1865) is the first mention of the word *slavery* in the Constitution, ending the practice at the national level. Slavery had been abolished in various states since the eighteenth century, but now it was terminated nationally, with Congress given the authority to enforce the ban. At a minimum, this meant that no one would any longer be a serf or a slave by reason of birth or inevitability. Former slaves were now recognized as born equal and free to pursue happiness. Clearly, the Thirteenth Amendment expanded the ideal of equality of opportunity to more Americans.

Similarly, the first mention of the word *equal* in the Constitution is in the Fourteenth Amendment (1868). Section I of the Amendment provides that no state shall "deny to any person within its jurisdiction the equal protection of the laws." Read literally, or narrowly, it underscores rights established by the Founders from the beginning. But, in fact, this amendment took on a much wider meaning as interpreted later by courts, giving the federal government a base from which to undertake positive steps, not just preventive ones, in pursuing equality.

Finally, the Fifteenth Amendment (1870) provided a federal right to vote regardless of "race, color, or previous condition of servitude." Again, this guarantee is reflective of the Founders' view that the people have the right to vote, but it clarified that it can no longer be denied to those who had not enjoyed it, and it also gave Congress the right to enforce this article.

These three so-called Civil War amendments shift the questions of liberty and equality away from the discretion of the states to the level of federal rights, guaranteed by the Constitution and enforced by Congress. Although a civil war was fought to make these rights possible, they were nevertheless constitutionalized by the deliberate sense of the community. As we look back from this bridge, these amendments may be understood as helping to complete the equality of the Founding. Or, looking ahead, they may be seen as part of a new nationalism on which Progressives would seek to build a different approach to equality of opportunity.

Lincoln's own Gettysburg Address reflected these dual understandings of the Civil War era and its amendments. On one hand, Lincoln looked back to the Founding, when the "new nation" was born in 1776, "conceived in Liberty, and dedicated to the proposition that all men are created equal." His challenge for the future was to make certain that "government of the people, by the people, for the people, shall not perish from the earth." All this sounds like a continuation of the Founders' work, with a nod to Benjamin Franklin's challenge, "a republic, if you can keep it." But Lincoln also suggests that something new has happened, opening the door to "a new birth of freedom." While the speech acknowledges that the nation was "conceived in Liberty," Lincoln also said it was "dedicated to the proposition that all men are created equal." Is Lincoln now elevating equality over freedom, or are they still twin goals? Is he looking toward a new nationalism, which the Progressives would embrace? In a sense, one can find support for both the Founding view of equality and the newer perspective of the Progressives, depending on how you read Lincoln's historic message.

Wilson, the Progressives, and a New Equality of Opportunity

Approximately a century after the Founding, the Progressives began calling out major changes in American life that, in their view, demanded concomitant changes in how we understand equality and, correspondingly, how the country should be governed. Franklin Roosevelt, one of our Progressive presidents, put it very succinctly in his historic address to the San Francisco Commonwealth Club on September 23, 1932, when he declared, "Equality of opportunity as we have known it no longer exists."

Just as the Founders' notions of political liberty and equality were in reaction against the monarchy and inequality of England and Europe, the Progressives' ideas of equality were born of the social climate they saw developing in America, especially during its period of industrialization. One might choose the year 1890 to demarcate the beginning of these profound changes in American society—a time when the US Census Bureau officially declared that the American frontier was now closed and no longer would it collect data tracking westward migration. Many social implications were thought to flow from this important demographic development.

As noted earlier, observers of equality in America found the availability of free land, or the open frontier, to be a significant contributor. This "frontier thesis" was developed and articulated by historian Frederick Jackson Turner, an academic at the University of Wisconsin. In 1893, Turner delivered a paper, "The Significance of the American Frontier in American History," at the annual meeting of the American Historical Association. In it he argued that key differences between Europeans and Americans had developed because of the physical environment of the New World, especially the availability of free land and the vast expanse of the continent that encouraged people to keep moving westward onto new frontiers. Turner continued his argument in "The Problem of the West" in 1896, noting that the availability of free land created new social conditions in the New World, in turn spawning a "freedom of opportunity" for "new activities, new lines of growth, new institutions and new ideals."[10]

With westward expansion having reached the Pacific Ocean, and the official closing of the frontier, Progressives argued that social conditions had now changed. Focusing on the industrial revolution in this same time period, Progressives argued that America was turning from its agrarian roots, with full opportunities available through farming on free land, to an urban, industrial society. Economist Richard T. Ely argued that these changes required "new economic and governmental directives to replace the frontier."[11]

A major Progressive thinker, Herbert Croly, captured much of the Progressive philosophy in his 1909 book, *The Promise of American Life*. In it, Croly argued that Americans had lived in a bit of a dream state for the past one hundred years, one in which individual economic interests could be pursued without harming, and perhaps even benefiting, the country. But now, Croly wrote, "the end of the harmony between economic individualism and national stability" created many "perplexities, confusions and dangers for the twentieth century."[12] In fact, Croly and the Progressives saw the seeds of these problems actually planted in the Founding itself. "Democracy as an idea was misunderstood" at the Founding, Croly wrote.[13] It was a narrow Jeffersonian view promoting individual interests that then was attached to states' rights, an "inadequate conception" of democracy and nationality that lasted until the Civil War.[14]

If the Progressives do go back in time for guidance or a point of departure, it would be to Lincoln and, according to Croly, his broader conception of democracy and nationality than that of the Founders. But then Croly takes away what he has given to Lincoln, saying what Lincoln meant by "all men are created equal" is best expressed today in the principle of "equal rights for all and special privileges for none." That legal understanding of equality was not good enough for contemporary society, Croly argued. It is in harmony with an equal start in the race but leads to an "unequal finish." According to Croly, Americans living in a legal system that holds "private property sacred" may favor "equal rights, but there cannot possibly be any equal opportunities for exercising such rights." Neither Madison nor Lincoln were offering what Theodore Roosevelt would later popularize as a "Square Deal."[15]

Now, according to Croly, there would need to be major government reforms to address the new social and economic circumstances of the country.[16] Such reform must be national, not merely state or local, and it would necessarily address the social problem: namely, the relation between capital and labor and the unequal distribution of wealth. To sum it up, "the government needs to be in the business of promoting social equality," Croly said.[17] Returning to the inadequacies of the Founding, Croly felt there needed to be a new Declaration of Independence based on social justice and a new declaration of emancipation from the doctrine of economic individualism.[18]

If Croly led the philosophical thinking of the Progressive revolution, politicians such as Theodore Roosevelt and Woodrow Wilson undertook its actual implementation. Having served as a Republican president from 1901 to 1909, Roosevelt formed a new Progressive Party and ran for president under its banner in 1912. His 1910 speech, "The New Nationalism," captured a healthy amount of this new Progressive thinking and touched on aspects of his Square Deal. Calling on the spirit of Abraham Lincoln, Roosevelt pointed out that one of the main objects, "and often the only object," in the struggle for human betterment has been "equality of opportunity." It is an economic conflict, Roosevelt thought, between "the men who possess more than they have earned and the men who have earned more than they possess." He felt it was necessary for the rules to change in order to provide a "square deal" and "more substantial equality of opportunity."

To Roosevelt this new push for equality of opportunity required freeing the government from the "sinister influence or control of special interests." It demanded government supervision of corporations, especially those forming illegal combinations and engaged in "unfair money-getting." Further, government must play a larger role in preventing "financial panics"; there should be greater regulation of labor markets. To do this, Roosevelt called for a new nationalism, one that could address these major new social and economic problems. The Progressive platform of 1912, under which Roosevelt ran for president, rolled out more of the particulars. These included undertaking the regulation of labor by the national government, with significant new rules about the workday, workweek, wages, and working conditions. Social insurance was needed, the platform claimed, to protect against the hardships of old age, sickness, and irregular employment. The emphasis on a new understanding of equality of opportunity required more government, and specifically more national government, with greater regulation and intervention into the economy and stronger social policies.

Although Roosevelt did not win the presidency in 1912, another Progressive (running as a Democrat) did: Woodrow Wilson. Prior to entering politics, Wilson had been an academic who carefully studied the operation of the federal government and the case for expanding its powers. As both president of Princeton University and subsequently governor of New Jersey, he advocated for reformist and Progressive policies. It was no surprise, then, that upon his inauguration as president of the United States in January 1913 Wilson would begin to implement his Progressive ideas on a national scale.

In his 1913 inaugural address, noting that the House, Senate, and presidency were all now in Democratic hands, Wilson said it was time to "count the human cost" of industrialization. Some had used industrialization for "private and selfish purposes" while others suffered. In particular, Wilson noted that there had not been sufficient attention to "the means by which government may be put at the service of humanity." He underscored that there "can be no equality of opportunity, the first essential in the body politic," if people are not "shielded . . . from the consequences of great industrial and social processes which they can not alter, control or singly cope with." Clearly, Wilson intended to put government more directly into the equality business, especially in economic and social terms, in this new industrial age.[19] What was needed was not only Teddy Roosevelt's Square Deal but also Wilson's "New Freedom" for government to act.

To accomplish these new goals Wilson felt it was time to move away from the limited federal government of the Founding and allow it to evolve toward a much more active and expansive role. "Governments are living things," he wrote in his 1908 book, *Constitutional Government in the United States*, "and operate as organic wholes. Moreover, governments have their natural evolution and are one thing in one age, another in another."[20] Wilson saw that the federal government needed to evolve in at least three significant ways: (1) by leaving behind limitations imposed by the Founders; (2) by taking up new responsibilities; and (3) by setting aside politics to operate as a new scientific, administrative state. In these ways, Wilson was prepared to launch a new, Progressive revolution in the operation of the federal government.

First, Wilson argued that it was time to leave the Founders' ideas of limited government behind. Wilson felt that the Founders' notions of checks and balances, for example, were too mechanistic for a modern government. He argued that they were "a sort of unconscious copy of the Newtonian theory of the universe," whereas today, he said, we should be organic, following Charles Darwin instead. Contrary to the Founders' desire to balance powers, which Wilson felt left governmental power divided, and hence "obscured" and therefore "irresponsible," Wilson thought it far better to have "large powers and unhampered discretion," which can be "easily watched and brought to book."

And what should this larger federal power now take up, according to Wilson? To be sure, the Progressive agenda of greater regulation of business and the economy to protect smaller businesses as well as the common man. This is what he described in his first inaugural address as shielding people from "great industrial and social processes" that they do not have the power on their own to alter or control. In an earlier time, Wilson claimed, we used to say, "Let every man look out for himself," but against the forces of industry and a larger and more powerful society, this is no longer enough. Then, too, Wilson argued it was time for government to play a direct role in helping Americans achieve equality of opportunity through social programs run by new agencies and administrators. He enacted a host of programs to help laborers, farmers, federal workers, and others—to the degree that he laid the foundation for what would become the welfare state.

In domestic policy, however, Wilson is perhaps best known for his advancement of a new, scientific administrative state to carry out the Progressive agenda. He described this as a new "Darwinian" approach to government, replacing the Founders' mechanistic and limited "Newtonian" systems. "Government," he said, "is not a machine, but a living thing. It falls, not under the theory of the universe, but under the theory of organic life. It is accountable to Darwin, not to Newton."[21] Having seen "every day new things which the state ought to do, the next thing is to see clearly how it ought to do them," Wilson wrote.[22]

To advance a new approach to government, Wilson said it would be necessary to look to Europe for the best ideas. America's time as "a new country" is over, he wrote, and now "we need to turn to Europe for guidance, not in constitution making but in administrative action."[23] Oddly, Wilson looked not to the French Revolution, as other Progressives had done, but to the firmer hand of monarchs and dictators such as Napoleon: "Napoleon succeeded the monarchs of France, to exercise a power as unrestricted as they had ever possessed." He admired how Napoleon had perfected "the civil machinery by the single will of an absolute ruler before the dawn of a constitutional era." Greater executive power over an expanding administrative state then was Wilson's formula for a new, Progressive government.

Wilson's thinking then took a leap away from government of, by, and for the people advanced by the Founders to a government led by enlightened administrators. And why not—since, according to Wilson, the people were "unphilosophical" and vote in "multifarious" ways. The *administration* of government, Wilson wrote, is "outside the proper sphere of *politics*. Administrative questions are not political questions." So, we are no longer worried about constitutional and political matters in a Wilsonian government, but how to administer an increasingly complex republic with more powerful executive leaders.

What we need, per Wilson, are good cooks. After all, Wilson wrote, "self-government does not consist in having a hand in everything, any more than housekeeping consists necessarily in cooking dinner with one's own hands. The cook must be trusted with a large discretion as to the management of the fires and ovens." Better government requires good cooks with broad discretion, "a body of thoroughly trained officials serving during good behavior." Such public service must be "removed from the common political life of the people" for "its motives, it objects, its policy, its standards must be bureaucratic."

In order to pursue equality of opportunity, then, Wilson advanced not interests checking interests, or ambition counteracting ambition—as the Founders had done—but rather powerful and scientific bureaucrats carrying out the right policies. The real power in a Wilson government should not be in the hands of the unthinking people or the corrupt politicians in Congress, but in the hands of enlightened administrators in the executive branch. Wilson began to grow the number and power of administrative agencies, creating the Federal Reserve, the Federal Trade Commission, the Internal Revenue Service, and the Department of Labor. He built on Theodore Roosevelt's antitrust agenda with the passage of the Clayton Act. As president, he began appearing before Congress for a State of the Union message outlining the president's legislative priorities and had his staff draft legislation, something heretofore left to Congress. Wilson also reformed and expanded the presidential veto power. The Progressive agenda now had an activist president and a powerful executive branch able to implement its ideas.

Progressive Constitutional Amendments

Even though Wilson felt the Progressive cause was best advanced by increasing the administrative power and scope of the executive branch, Progressives nevertheless enacted four amendments to the Constitution to advance their cause. Some increased the power of the executive branch, but all advanced the Progressive agenda.

The Sixteenth Amendment, adopted in 1913, established the power of Congress to impose a federal income tax. If the federal government was to grow in power and influence in response to the industrial age, it would need its own source of funding, and the Sixteenth Amendment assured that. Importantly, this power also gave Congress the ability to adopt a progressive income tax, assessing those at the top of the income scale a higher tax than those further down the ladder. This direct tax—as compared with indirect taxes previously relied upon—soon became the federal government's primary source of revenue. As scholars have pointed out, the Sixteenth Amendment "forever changed the character of the United States government from a modest central government to the much more powerful modern government."[24] If the modern mantra, "follow the money," is a key to understanding power, the Sixteenth Amendment was the most important of the Progressive amendments and constituted, in the spirit of Wilson, a major strengthening of federal government administration.

The Seventeenth Amendment, also adopted in 1913, was of a different character; it removed the power of state legislatures to elect US senators and gave it directly to the people. It was Progressive in the sense that it removed the election of senators from the political and sometimes corrupt legislative process against which Wilson and other Progressives had railed. But the direct election of senators also undid one of the Founders' balances of power, removing state power in favor of giving greater power to the people. It continues to be a progressive policy today to remove structures imposed by the Founders to create balances and separations of power in favor of more direct democracy.

The Nineteenth Amendment (1920) extended the right to vote to women. This, of course, is a classic case of extending equality of opportunity with which Progressives and conservatives would, by now, both agree. Progressives were especially in favor of this at the time as part of their larger package of concerns about labor and working conditions. In addition to advancing voting rights, the Progressive nature of women's suffrage also launched a long and continuing expansion of not only women's rights and privileges, but of civil rights more broadly.

Finally, the Eighteenth Amendment (1920), or Prohibition, is more difficult to explain as a Progressive priority. Telling people how to live—or not live—their lives does not enhance liberty, or people's equal opportunity. Perhaps it could be explained as an effort to undo business interests that were preying on people's proclivity to abuse alcohol. Critics of the Progressive movement might argue that it is an example of its interest in using big government to control how people conduct their own affairs. It may be seen as an example of the Progressive view that human nature can be changed and, indeed, changed by government—contrary to the Madisonian view that human nature must be understood by government as fixed. In any event, it did not work, and by popular demand, it was removed from the Constitution in 1933, making it the only amendment to be overturned.

Although the Progressive-versus-conservative debate launched in this era has continued for one hundred years and still counting, it was not primarily carried out by constitutional amendment. In fact, as noted in chapter 2, President Franklin Roosevelt's entire New Deal was undertaken without a single constitutional amendment. The Progressive strategy moved primarily through administrative agencies and executive power, supported by decisions in the federal courts.

The Brief "Return to Normalcy" in the 1920s

Before we turn to the revolutionary New Deal of the 1930s, it is worth noting that a series of more conservative presidents attempted to turn back the Progressive tide in the 1920s, with only limited success. History reminds us that, at the same time as Wilson's Progressive reforms, America was engaged in World War I on the international front. Major wars inevitably lead to increases in government spending and federal power, so along with Wilson's Progressive agenda, there was a kind of double push in that direction. Three Republican presidents of the 1920s—Warren G. Harding, Calvin Coolidge, and Herbert Hoover—sought to push back against bigger and more powerful government and return things to normal.

Warren G. Harding ran for the presidency in 1920 calling for a "return to normalcy." In his campaign speech of that title, Harding said, "all human ills are not curable by legislation," and the "quantity of statutory enactment and excess of government offer no substitute for quality of citizenship." He argued that "problems of maintained civilization are not to be solved by a transfer of responsibility from citizenship to government." In his inaugural address, he warned, "Our most dangerous tendency is to expect too much of government." In that same message, Harding observed, "No one may justly deny the equality of opportunity that made us what we are," yet his path to that was a return to normal business and government. Yes, Harding sought to put "the fevered delirium of war" behind America, but he was also concerned with the growth in federal bureaucracy and regulation in an attempt to use government to create greater equality.

Calvin Coolidge succeeded Harding in 1923 and he worked diligently, and in painstaking detail, to trim federal spending back to pre–World War I levels. Coolidge was on the side of the Founders, believing as they did that equality was a result of shared humanity, not government programs.[25] Coolidge attacked the Progressive argument that it was time to move beyond the government of the Founders, noting that the Declaration of Independence was in reality the last word on fundamental questions of freedom and equality.[26] Coolidge felt that removing self-reliance from the people in favor of greater government intervention and regulation was moving America in precisely the wrong direction.[27] Coolidge presided over a huge period of economic growth, which increased opportunities widely.

Finally, Herbert Hoover became president in 1929, pressing his case for "rugged individualism" accompanied by equality of opportunity. Indeed, as will be described in chapter 2, the Herbert Hoover–Franklin Roosevelt debates of the 1930s bring the conservative-versus-Progressive debates over equality of opportunity into sharp focus.

Conclusion

The Founders or the Progressives? Madison or Wilson? Or perhaps we are required to accept some compromise of the two? Which view of equality of opportunity will be the basis for American domestic policy in the twentieth and now twenty-first century? That is still very much the debate today. As the

Founders stated in the Declaration, "all men are created equal," and, armed with individual liberty, Americans were free to pursue equality of opportunity as they saw fit. It was the role of government to defend these political freedoms through the constitutional republic created by the Constitution.

To all this, the Progressives said that that might have been sufficient in the eighteenth century, but equality of opportunity in the nineteenth and twentieth centuries required more of government. With the closing of the American frontier and the arrival of the industrial revolution, American rugged individualism was no longer enough. People had to prepare to live in closer quarters in urban areas, requiring both more government regulation and assistance. The federal government needed to play a much larger role in the economy, in the regulation of business, and in social programs to aid those less able to provide for themselves. This, the Progressives argued, was the new path to equality of opportunity: more government, more regulation, and greater security.

In his book *The Conservative Sensibility*, George Will correctly argues that the whole liberal-versus-conservative debate today boils down to whose model we follow: the Founders' or the Progressives'.[28] He argues that what conservatives seek to conserve is the Founding, whereas Wilson and the Progressives find Madison's ideas anachronistic and out of touch. It is this debate, and the policies its proponents sought to implement, that we now follow in the modern era, from the New Deal of Franklin Roosevelt, to the Great Society of Lyndon Johnson, through the Reagan Revolution of the 1980s, to today. And then we ask the question: For the future, is there room for both the Founders and the Progressives as we pursue equality of opportunity, or must we choose only one or the other?

Notes

1. Valuable original source material can be found in Philip B. Kurland and Ralph Lerner, eds., *The Founders' Constitution*, 5 vols. (Chicago: University of Chicago Press, 1987), and F. N. Thorpe, ed., *The Federal and State Constitutions* (Washington, DC: Government Printing Office, 1909).

2. George W. Carey and James McClellan, eds., *The Federalist* (Indianapolis, IN: Liberty Fund, Inc., 2001), 46.

3. Carey and McClellan, 173.

4. Carey and McClellan, 288.

5. Madison letter to Jacob De La Motta, 1820.

6. Benjamin Franklin, "Information to Those Who Would Come to America," *Writings* 8 (September 1782): 603–14, in Kurland and Lerner, *The Founders' Constitution*, vol. 1, 531–34.

7. J. Hector St. John de Crèvecoeur, *Letters from an American Farmer* (New York: 1904), 49–56.

8. Alexis de Tocqueville, *Democracy in America*, ed. Harvey C. Mansfield and Delba Winthrop (Chicago: University of Chicago Press, 2002), 488.

9. Abigail Adams to John Adams, March 31, 1776, in Kurland and Lerner, *Founders' Constitution*, vol. 1, *Major Themes*, 518.

10. Frederick Jackson Turner, "The Problem of the West," *Atlantic Monthly* 78 (September 1896): 289–97.

11. David M. Wrobel, *The End of American Exceptionalism: Frontier Anxiety from the Old West to the New Deal* (Lawrence, KS: University Press of Kansas, 1993), 74.

12. David W. Levy, *Herbert Croly of the New Republic: The Life and Thought of an American Progressive* (Princeton, NJ: Princeton University Press, 1985), 97.

13. Herbert David Croly, *The Promise of American Life* (1909; repr., New York: BiblioBazaar, 2006), 42.

14. Croly, 51, 59–60.

15. Croly, 183–86.

16. Croly, 100.

17. Croly, 195.

18. Croly, 266–72, 415, 421.

19. Henry Steele Commager, ed., *Documents of American History* (Englewood, NJ: Prentice Hall, 1968), vol. 2 of 2, *Documents of American History since 1865*, 82–84.

20. Woodrow Wilson, *Constitutional Government in the United States* (New York: The Columbia University Press, 1908).

21. Wilson, chapter 3.

22. Woodrow Wilson, "The Study of Administration," in *Woodrow Wilson: The Essential Political Writings*, ed. Ronald J. Pestritto (Lanham, MD: Lexington Books, 2005), 234.

23. Wilson, 234.

24. Joseph R. Fishkin, William E. Forbath, and Erik M. Jensen, "The Sixteenth Amendment," *Interactive Constitution*, National Constitution Center, https://constitutioncenter.org/interactive-constitution/interpretation/amendment-xvi/interps/139.

25. Calvin Coolidge, *The Price of Freedom* (New York: Scribner's Sons, 1924), 233.

26. Joseph Postell, "Calvin Coolidge: Forefather of Our Conservatism," Heritage Foundation Report, February 20, 2013, https://www.heritage.org/political-process/report/calvin-coolidge-forefather-our-conservatism.

27. Postell.

28. George F. Will, *The Conservative Sensibility* (New York: Hachette Books, 2019).

CHAPTER TWO

Franklin Roosevelt's New Deal

*"Equality of Opportunity as We Have
Known It No Longer Exists"*

The 1932 presidential campaign, pitting Franklin Roosevelt against the incumbent Herbert Hoover in the throes of the Great Depression, ushered in revolutionary change to America. Roosevelt's New Deal transformed the span of what the federal government did, as well as how it operated, and became the paradigm for American domestic and economic policy for the next 85 years and still counting. As we have argued elsewhere, the New Deal was America's French Revolution, seeking to transform everything.[1]

Although it has received relatively little attention, one issue in that historic campaign—the debate over equality of opportunity—has turned out to be of lasting importance. Herbert Hoover's "rugged individualism" (a term he coined in his 1928 presidential campaign) was always accompanied by equality of opportunity, in contrast with various forms of European individualism with their systems of class and caste. Roosevelt and his New Dealers challenged not only Hoover but specifically his notions of individualism and equality of opportunity. In fact, in his famous Commonwealth Club speech in San Francisco during the campaign, Roosevelt said directly: "Equality of opportunity as we have known it no longer exists." The Hoover-Roosevelt debate over equality of opportunity—what it means, whether it exists, and whether it required dramatic change—became a turning point in America's understanding of this fundamental doctrine.

The Historic Hoover-Roosevelt Debates

Franklin Roosevelt, the challenger, and Herbert Hoover, the incumbent, waged an important war of ideas during their 1932 presidential campaigns. Hoover captured the scope and significance of the battle when he said in a speech at Madison Square Garden near the end of the campaign: "This campaign is more than a contest between two men. It is more than a contest between two parties. It is a contest between two philosophies of government." The Hoover-Roosevelt exchanges were not debates in the way that Abraham Lincoln and Stephen Douglas debated face to face or, a century later, when Richard Nixon met John Kennedy in the first televised "joint appearance" of candidates. They certainly were not the one-minute sound bites that candidates who take the stage with fifteen primary opponents must deliver today. Theirs were clashing ideas developed in speeches delivered in a back-and-forth sort of extended correspondence, one with both a contemporary audience and now the deeper perspective of history.

As the challenger, Roosevelt was the protagonist in these debates, proposing bold new ideas to counter the Great Depression that had savaged the American economy and put millions out of work. Indeed, Roosevelt's fundamental principle was less a series of policy prescriptions than a mandate to try something, almost anything, new. In a speech at Oglethorpe University on May 22, 1932, he called for "bold, persistent experimentation." "Above all," Roosevelt said, "try something." Importantly, Roosevelt believed such experiments should be led by the federal government, a dramatic change in how the economy would be run. Roosevelt offered a "New Deal" in which "the forgotten man" would become the object of national planning.

Roosevelt was an early practitioner of the Rahm Emanuel school of public policy. As chief of staff to President Barack Obama, Emanuel said in 2012, "You never want a serious crisis to go to waste. . . . It's an opportunity to do things . . .

you could not do before."[2] It was Roosevelt's intention to use the crisis of the Great Depression to implement a host of social ideas and economic policies that Progressives had been developing for decades. The Great Depression was the moment, and Roosevelt was the man to initiate a revolution in American economic and social policy, while also expanding dramatically the role of the federal government, and especially the presidency.

Herbert Hoover was on the defensive with Roosevelt, seeking to preserve his ideal of ordered liberty in the face of the Great Depression as well as Roosevelt's own assault. It must have been an awkward position for Hoover, who had sometimes been regarded as a Progressive himself. When Hoover returned to the US from leading food relief efforts in Europe following World War I, both parties sought him as a presidential candidate and Roosevelt himself spoke favorably of Hoover. As historian David Kennedy pointed out, "Hoover was no mossback conservative in the Harding-Coolidge mold."[3] Yet Roosevelt during the campaign, as well as historians later, portrayed Hoover as tied to an old form of laissez-faire capitalism, someone who would not take sufficient government action to tackle the Great Depression and help those who were suffering from it. If Roosevelt was seeking government intervention into the economy and greater social justice, Hoover maintained that the American system did not require any kind of radical transformation in order to survive an economic emergency. Having lived many years abroad and watched Europe give in to various forms of totalitarianism, Hoover had come to believe very strongly in the American system of individualism coupled with equality of opportunity.

Thus, the stage was set for a robust debate on the future course of America: Would the country turn toward greater government intervention in the name of social justice, or would it continue to emphasize liberty and individualism? Was the Great Depression, as Roosevelt felt, an expression of a larger set of challenges to which the federal government would need to respond, or was it a temporary crisis that demanded no fundamental change to the American system and way of governing, as Hoover believed? In particular, what about the role of equality of opportunity in America? Had circumstances changed such that it was no longer available to the American people, as they had historically experienced it, as Roosevelt claimed? Was it, therefore, necessary for government to step in to create and guarantee such equality? Or was Hoover on sound footing when he asserted that equality of opportunity—what he called "the fair chance of Abraham Lincoln"—continued to be at the heart of the American system? The answers to these questions would establish a course for the nation.

The Hoover-Roosevelt debates took place in two discrete periods. The first was during the 1932 presidential campaign itself, when the candidates laid out their visions and issued attacks on their opponent. Less well known, however, is the even more robust debate that occurred after Roosevelt assumed the presidency and the New Deal appeared in full bloom. In these later debates, Hoover became the protagonist, aggressively attacking what he regarded as the excesses of the New Deal. Indeed, as both historian George Nash and we have pointed out, Hoover became a full-throated conservative during the Roosevelt presidency and his attacks on the New Deal framed the ongoing debate between progressives and conservatives today.[4]

Roosevelt's Attack on Equality of Opportunity

In a sweeping campaign address to San Francisco's Commonwealth Club on September 23, 1932, Franklin Roosevelt made a shocking assertion: "Equality of opportunity as we have known it no longer exists." This was no mere random observation but rather a direct challenge to Herbert Hoover, who had constantly preached the central importance of equality of opportunity. Now, according to Roosevelt, it was dead. Yet several questions remained: How and when did it die; what did Roosevelt mean by "as we have known it"; and, could it be revived, or would it be replaced by something else? To answer these questions requires both a careful look at the whole of the historic Commonwealth Club speech as well as the broader thinking of Roosevelt and his brain trust of advisors.

The Commonwealth Club address has been included among the top one hundred speeches in American rhetoric.[5] It provides a thorough accounting of the Progressive view of American economic history and argues for a radical redefinition of the role of the federal government in the marketplace. As historian David Kennedy wrote: "As much as any single document can, that speech served as a charter for the New Deal's economic program."[6] It was, as other historians put it, "the New Deal manifesto."[7]

The text of the speech was drafted by Professor Adolf A. Berle Jr., a member of Roosevelt's brain trust, and his wife, Beatrice, under the title, "The New Individualism."[8] Berle himself was a controversial figure, having coauthored *The Modern Corporation and Private Property*, which purported to show how major corporations, along with their directors and banks, controlled the American economy.[9] One of Roosevelt's key advisors, Rexford Tugwell, has asserted that, in the busy travel schedule of the campaign, Berle's draft was only lightly reviewed late in the day by primary policy and speech advisor Raymond Moley, and in turn Roosevelt saw it only the night before delivery in the hotel, resulting in a mere handful of modest corrections.[10]

Berle's book, cowritten with Gardiner C. Means, described how wealthy barons had dominated the economy, shrinking opportunities for average Americans. Berle thought Herbert Hoover had handed Roosevelt an important campaign issue by his constant emphasis on individualism and equality of opportunity. "What he means," Berle wrote to Roosevelt in a memorandum, is that "the government shall keep clear of the entire economic system, confining itself to emergency relief, keeping the peace, and the like."[11] In fact, Berle argued, the dominance of the economy by business titans had effectively destroyed both individualism and equality of opportunity. Instead, Berle proposed "a far truer individualism," which meant that "government acted as regulating and unifying agency, so that within the framework of this industrial system, individual men and women could survive, have homes, educate their children, and so forth."[12] To Berle, a "new individualism" meant that individuals might survive and prosper only to the extent that the government undertook aggressive regulation of business.

The speech acknowledges that there was an earlier time when individualism and equal opportunity existed without systemic government regulation. In the days of the Western frontier, Roosevelt conceded, "land was substantially free" and "so great were our natural resources" that people could keep moving west to stake out new ground and a productive way of life. Admittedly, Roosevelt acknowledged, "the happiest of economic conditions made that day long and splendid."

Now, Roosevelt continued in his Commonwealth Club address, the American economy presented new challenges that demanded a greater role for government. Now, "a new force was released . . . called the industrial revolution," and government, which heretofore had "merely been called upon to produce conditions within which people could live happily, labor peacefully, and rest secure," must now "aid in the consummation" of the people's dreams. Whereas during the "period of expansion, there was equal opportunity for all," now we had reached "our last frontier," with "no more free land" and industry so uncontrolled that "opportunity would no longer be equal" and big business could now "threaten the economic freedom of individuals to earn a living." This new day with its fresh challenges "clearly . . . calls for a re-appraisal of values," Roosevelt concluded. "The day of the Financial Titan is over," he claimed, and "the day of enlightened administration has come."

The Problems: The Closing of the American Frontier and Industrialization

One central tenet of Roosevelt's assertion that America had entered a new era—one that rendered Herbert Hoover's rugged individualism coupled with equality of opportunity inoperative—was the closing of the American frontier. Progressives, including Roosevelt and his advisors, had embraced a theory developed by University of Wisconsin scholar Frederick Jackson Turner that the American West had been a powerful force shaping not only geography but also culture.[13] In a speech to the American Historical Association in 1893, Turner argued that European settlers became true Americans through an "exceptional" evolutionary process of traveling from the East Coast across the American frontier. Conquering free land, coupled with the hardship and adventure of travel, developed key features of the American character such as individualism, egalitarianism, and materialism. The French journalist Alexis de Tocqueville had recognized these features in his earlier book, *Democracy in America*, noting that equality and democracy were forged on the American frontier.[14]

Progressives also argued that 1920s Republican presidents Warren Harding, Calvin Coolidge, and Herbert Hoover had adopted notions of laissez-faire government that had been enabled by the economic growth and equality of opportunity available on the American frontier. *Laissez-faire*, from the French, means to leave alone or allow to do; when applied to government it refers to the theory that government only does those things that are indispensable, leaving individuals and markets free to do other things. With free land and equality of opportunity available further west, the demand for government regulation of business, economic, and social matters had not been great. By the late nineteenth century, however, laissez-faire had become associated with a society that did not care about people who lived on the margins; and it is surely this attack that Herbert Hoover resisted.

With the closing of the American frontier in 1890—when the US Census Bureau stopped counting migration to the West—Progressives argued that America was now confronted by fresh realities that demanded a different role for government. In the Commonwealth Club address, Roosevelt pointed out that his distant cousin, President Theodore Roosevelt, had seen how industrial power had grown and consolidated in such a way as to create "danger that opportunity would no longer be equal," and "in that hour, our antitrust laws were born." Now, according to FDR, "our industrial plant is built," perhaps even "overbuilt," and great corporations have seized the economic initiative, leaving little room for the small, independent businessman. Roosevelt then delivered another bold pronouncement, or what he called "a re-appraisal of values": "A mere builder of more industrial plants, a creator of more railroad systems, an organizer of more corporations, is as likely to be a danger as a help. The day of the great promoter or the financial Titan," he continued, "is over." The task now is no longer building great businesses, but "of administering resources and plants already in hand." In other words, we need to worry less about growing the pie and take up the task of dividing it fairly. This, of course, was now to be the work of government: to engage in "modifying and controlling our economic units."

The writings of other Progressives of the time, including many of Roosevelt's own advisors, reinforce the view that, with the closing of the American frontier and the arrival of industrialization, bold government regulation of business and intervention into the economy were necessary to assure equality of opportunity for "the forgotten man." Typical was New York University professor Henry Steele Commager's August 1933 essay, "Farewell to Laissez-Faire," calling for a "repudiation" of individualism and laissez-faire and an adjustment of America's "legal machinery to the demands of a new order."[15] Harold Ickes, who served as Roosevelt's Secretary of Interior, wrote that the frontier had led to the exploitation of people and natural resources and that government should now take "a sense of responsibility for the health, safety and well-being of the people."[16] The view was broadly held among Roosevelt and his advisors that ordinary Americans needed protection by a federal government that would become much more active in planning the economy, rather than leaving matters to the inefficiency and unfairness of markets.

In addition to the explicit arguments that they saw the closing of the frontier and the arrival of industrialization as damaging equality of opportunity, there was also an implicit belief among some of Roosevelt's advisors that the economy had hit its peak and begun to shrink. In their view, the Great Depression was merely a symptom of two larger problems: at best, markets were no longer able to allocate resources effectively and, worse, the economy itself had grown stagnant, perhaps permanently so. In the Commonwealth Club speech, Roosevelt alluded to the first issue as "the problem of underconsumption" which, in turn, required "distributing wealth and products more equitably," concluding that as a consequence, "the day of enlightened administration has come." Political scientist Donald Brand put it even more clearly: "According to New Deal reformers, the Great Depression was not a temporary aberration in the growth of national wealth associated with capitalism, it revealed emergent failures in markets as mechanisms for allocating economic resources in modern times."[17]

Others in the Roosevelt camp felt the problem was even deeper, that the economy itself had peaked and moved from abundance to scarcity. Progressive

Herbert Croly, for example, argued that now that "scarcity" was an issue, a national and socializing approach was necessary.[18] Roosevelt economist Lauchlin Currie wrote later, in 1939, "The violence of the depression following 1929 obscured for some time the fact that a profound change of a chronic or secular nature occurred," namely the emergence of a "mature" economy that had lost most of its capacity for growth.[19] This assumption would underlie Roosevelt's basic stance as a social justice warrior that it was time to worry less about growing a moribund economy and time for government to be sure that wealth was more equitably shared.

Herbert Hoover's Defense: Rugged Individualism

A decade earlier, in 1922, Herbert Hoover published a thoughtful essay, "American Individualism," setting out his understanding of what he called "the American system." Having lived much of his early career as a successful mining engineer abroad, leading major projects in Australia and China and then overseeing food relief in Europe during and following World War I, Hoover returned home with a deeper appreciation for America and its blessings of liberty in comparison with the many forms of totalitarianism he had witnessed abroad. Although Hoover would elaborate on his thinking during the 1928 presidential campaign, this essay was widely praised and is foundational to Hoover's understanding of equality of opportunity.[20]

Hoover pointed out in this essay that "five or six great social philosophies are at struggle in the world for ascendency," among those what he called "the Individualism of America." This is quite different from the individualism of Europe, Hoover said, with its systems of "castes and classes." By contrast, Hoover described America's approach as a "progressive individualism," one that does not "run riot" but that has at its heart "the tempering principle" of "equality of opportunity." America's progressive individualism is not the mere "legalistic justice based upon contracts, property and political equality," since it "long since abandoned the laissez-faire of the Eighteenth Century—the notion that it is 'every man for himself and the devil take the hindmost.'" All that was left behind when we "adopted the fair chance of Abraham Lincoln," making equality of opportunity "our most precious social ideal."

Although Hoover believed legal or constitutional equality was necessary, he did not argue they were sufficient. America was also committed to social equality, from the elimination of the class systems of Europe to Lincoln's efforts to end slavery in the New World. Further, Hoover embraced "the fair chance of Abraham Lincoln." Lincoln often referred to the race of life and the importance of people having a fair and equal opportunity to run it. In President Lincoln's first message to Congress on July 4, 1861, he spoke of the need "to elevate the condition of men—to lift artificial weights from all shoulders—to clear the paths of laudable pursuit for all—to afford all, an unfettered start, and a fair chance, in the race of life." He reinforced this message in his address to the 166th Ohio Regiment on August 22, 1864, when he spoke of "an open field and a fair chance for your industry, enterprise and intelligence; that you may all have equal privileges in the race of life." This view was what Hoover embraced.

Also fundamental to Hoover's understanding of individualism coupled with equality of opportunity was the growing abundance America had to share. Indeed, he argued that the days of the "pioneer are not over." To the surprise of some, perhaps, Hoover acknowledged concern in his essay with "equitable sharing of the product," but his solution was to increase the product for everyone as opposed to involving the government in distributing a fixed product. Socialism, he said, has proven to be "an economic and spiritual fallacy." He saw the problem of "large capital," but sought to instill in its holders "a spirit of community responsibility" and also "cooperation." His approach was one of stewardship, rather than a heavy hand of government regulation and distribution policies.

During the campaign, Hoover's primary response to Roosevelt's attacks on his notions of equality of opportunity and individualism came in his Madison Square Garden speech on October 31, 1932. One could summarize Hoover's defense with a simple question: Do we really need to destroy, or even radically change, the American system in order to address an economic emergency? Hoover felt that Roosevelt's New Deal proposals would "alter the whole foundations of our national life," and "destroy the very foundations of our American system." Hoover feared that Roosevelt's approach would grow the size, power, and role of the federal government in such a way as to break down the genius of federalism and the role of states and individuals in the republic. These "gigantic" increases in the federal government would themselves "break down the savings, the wages, the equality of opportunity among our people."

In his Madison Square Garden address, Hoover specifically challenged Roosevelt's bold Commonwealth Club speech, quoting the portions about our industrial plant having been completed and our last frontier reached, with our task now for the government to adapt economic organizations to the service of the people. Hoover pointed out both the errors in Roosevelt's approach and its misplaced pessimism about America's future. "I challenge the whole idea that we have ended the advance of America, that this country has reached the zenith of its power, the height of its development," Hoover said. He characterized Roosevelt's call to action as based on a "counsel of despair for the future of America" and a belief that we "have begun the decline and fall." Hoover believed that economic growth and new frontiers had been vital in developing equality of opportunity and that the fundamental underpinnings of growth were not destroyed by an economic depression.

The Solution: Two Paths to Equality of Opportunity

Roosevelt's and Hoover's very different diagnoses of the nature of the equality of opportunity problem prepared the way for fundamentally different paths toward addressing it. In Roosevelt's view, equality of opportunity in America had been built on a base that was no longer viable: free land, western expansion, the American frontier, and an agricultural economy. With industrialization and the closing of the American frontier, people could no longer expect to make their own way toward equality of opportunity. Instead, the government would need to become its guarantor, beating back industrial combinations, regulating business and the markets, and ensuring more equitable distribution of wealth. One could say that Roosevelt's understanding of equality of opportunity was less a legal or constitutional one and more one based on economics and social policy.

Moreover, the Great Depression was not a temporary problem to be solved, but a symptom of larger issues that required, or at least justified, radical surgery to strengthen the federal government and expand its role.

Hoover, on the other hand, felt the American system was essentially strong and would survive the Great Depression without fundamental change. To him, the foundation of equality of opportunity was in the permanent guarantees and structure of America's constitutional system and not based on the vagaries of a changing economy. In his nomination address to the Republican Convention in 1928, Hoover had traced this to the founders and the Declaration of Independence when they "propounded the revolutionary doctrine that all men are created equal and all should have equality before the law." This could only be done, Hoover said in his 1932 nomination address, by preserving "the fundamental principles of our social and economic system . . . founded upon a conception of ordered freedom. The test of that freedom is that there should be maintained equality of opportunity to every individual."

In his campaign messages, Roosevelt argued that the federal government needed to undertake a host of new regulations and initiatives in order to restore the equality of opportunity that had been lost in the closing of the frontier and the advent of the industrial age. A focal point for Roosevelt's plans was to place "the forgotten man" at the center of all government planning for the economy. In an April 7, 1932, campaign radio address, Roosevelt provided his introduction to this theme: "These unhappy times call for the building of plans that rest upon the forgotten, the unorganized, but the indispensable units of economic power . . . that build from the bottom up . . . that put their faith once more in the forgotten man at the bottom of the economic pyramid." Roosevelt complained that Hoover had been providing support for the banks and corporations, whereas "the objective of Government" should be to support "the little fellow." This would be accomplished, he said, by restoring buying power and providing economic assistance directly to the forgotten man.

The following month, on May 22, 1932, Roosevelt spoke to the graduating students at Oglethorpe University, pointing out that they were not going to be better off than they were when they entered four years earlier because so-called leaders of finance had not properly controlled and managed the economy. Instead, they relied optimistically on free markets, with "a lack of plan and a great waste." Our economy, Roosevelt claimed, has been characterized by "haphazardness . . . and gigantic waste," and now demanded "greater foresight and a larger measure of social planning." Roosevelt's turn toward a different kind of New Deal progressivism emphasized not more capital and production but rather thinking more about the consumer and bringing about a "more equitable distribution of the national income." Although it was a bold call, it was not accompanied at this point by a lot of specifics, with Roosevelt satisfied to demand "bold, persistent experimentation" to accomplish it. Nevertheless, a move for government to have a hand in the distribution of wealth was clearly signaled.

Finally, in an address in Boston on October 31, 1932, Roosevelt laid out more clearly how he would protect the forgotten man and his right to equality of opportunity. He acknowledged the need for immediate aid to address the crisis at hand, saying, "No citizen should be permitted to starve." Contrasting his approach to that of Herbert Hoover, who was reluctant to see the federal government take over direct relief that he thought should be the responsibility of charities along with local and state governments, Roosevelt said the "Federal Government owes the positive duty of stepping into the breach." Looking ahead, however, Roosevelt said we needed more "advance planning" for full employment and the economy. He advocated "a program of long-range planning," because to do any less "would be to misread the lessons of the depression."

Although further details would come later, Roosevelt's approach to restoring equality of opportunity was sketched clearly in the campaign. The federal government had a responsibility not just to the engines of the economic system, but to the end users, the consumers, the forgotten man. That duty included not just short-term relief, but a long-term plan to manage the economy and not leave it to the vagaries of free markets. The goal of his New Deal should be a fairer distribution of wealth and a better planned industrial and economic system carried out by the federal government itself.

If Roosevelt's agenda was to restore an equality of opportunity that he felt the average American had lost, Hoover's was to maintain equality of opportunity that he believed was still viable. If Roosevelt's path to restoring equality of opportunity traveled primarily down economic and social roads, Hoover saw all that as undoing the American constitutional and economic system and, with it, any future for equality of opportunity. Hoover, then, was determined both to show the viability of equality of opportunity under the present American system, and to show how the radical nature of Roosevelt's New Deal would completely undermine the foundation of ordered liberty, individualism, and equality of opportunity on which the country had been built. A clash of ideas, indeed.

When Hoover was first nominated for the presidency in 1928, his acceptance speech on August 11 placed emphasis on equality of opportunity and its place deep in the heart of the American system. The agenda he pursued in this speech was one of continuing to move the federal government away from the heavier role it played during World War I, pointing out that it was the "duty of government to avoid regulation as long as equal opportunity to all citizens is not invaded and public rights violated." Mentioning equality of opportunity no less than six times, he called it "the fundamental principle of our nation" but also asserted that protecting it for every citizen "is the negation of socialism." Therefore, to Hoover the notion of equal opportunity required standing against both excessive government regulation and socialism. He reminded his listeners that this equality went back to the Declaration's claim that "all men are created equal" and was carried out through our constitutional and economic systems.

In that same address, Hoover elaborated on his understanding of equality of opportunity through the metaphor of the race of life. "We, through free and universal education, provide the training of the runners," he said, adding that "we give to them the equal start," with "government the umpire of fairness in the race." But socialism, he warned, "bids an end to the race equally. It holds back the speedy to the pace of the slowest." Hoover went so far as to say that equality of opportunity is the test of all government policies.

Hoover again took issue with the pessimism expressed in Roosevelt's Commonwealth Club speech, arguing that America had not reached its final frontier or the end of its economic growth. "I do challenge the whole idea that we have ended the advance of America," Hoover said, "that this country has reached the zenith of its power, the height of its development. . . . I deny that the promise of American life has been fulfilled, for that means we have begun the decline and fall." Instead, Hoover argued that the American spirit was still alive and we are "on the frontiers of development and of invention." The danger, he pointed out, was the growth of bureaucracy that threatened our freedoms and opportunities. This, he claimed, will create not free people but rather "regimentation." Hoover's dream was an America "where men and women may walk in ordered liberty" leading to greater and greater opportunity.

Hoover was correct to say that the election of 1932 was more than a contest between two men, but rather a contest between two philosophies of government. Unfortunately for Hoover, voters are not philosophers, and they are far more likely to cast their ballots based on short-term matters such as an economic emergency than on longer-term questions of ideology. Given different economic circumstances, voters might well have agreed with Hoover that it was not necessary to change the entire American system to address an economic emergency. But given massive unemployment and starvation, American voters wanted change. It was one of those elections like that faced later in the century by Bill Clinton when his political advisor James Carville said, "It's the economy, stupid." Indeed, it was, and Hoover lost the 1932 election in a landslide. Roosevelt could say that they chose his ideas of government growing to oversee, regulate, and plan the economy over Hoover's old-fashioned ideas about ordered liberty, individualism, and opportunity. If not a voter mandate, that certainly became the reality as the New Deal rolled out.

The New Deal and Hoover's Response

As Roosevelt implemented his New Deal, Hoover continued the debate from the sidelines, sharpening the argument about equality of opportunity as well as other topics. He had intended a quiet post-presidency, saying when he returned to California: "On economic and policy questions I am silent. . . . Even on fishing I am silent."[21] He maintained his silence for nearly two years but finally, frustrated by the direction of the New Deal, he began a national speaking tour in February 1935, which, by the time of the Republican National Convention in June 1936, saw him delivering addresses covering forty-five thousand miles in twenty-eight states.

As we have argued elsewhere, Roosevelt's New Deal changed many things, including Herbert Hoover himself. Hoover turned from a mild-mannered progressive republican to a full-throated conservative on the warpath over the excesses of the New Deal.[22] Hoover biographer George Nash discovered the manuscript of a book Hoover had worked on documenting his "crusade" against the New Deal.[23] This time Hoover was the protagonist, able to put the policies of the New Deal under attack rather than defending his own record. But it is never quite the same to be contending as a former president, and in some ways Hoover's was a voice crying in the wilderness. Still, he was making important arguments, including claims about equality of opportunity, that still resonate, making these continuing debates very much a foreshadowing of progressive and conservative debates today.

Roosevelt used the presidency to pursue his equality of opportunity agenda, both implementing actual programs from his campaign while also expanding the underlying philosophical case for equality. By the end of his historic term, he had accomplished revolutionary increases in government regulation of business and management of the economy in the name of establishing equality for his forgotten man. However, the more he achieved, the more he wanted, so much so that he ultimately made a case for new economic freedoms and guarantees as a kind of social justice warrior. All of this effected a new baseline for the American welfare state, upon which later presidents have continued to build.

Roosevelt's first hundred days in office carried out a legislative revolution, accompanied by executive orders, the likes of which had not been seen before or since. In addition to emergency measures to close the banks and create jobs, Roosevelt began a longer-term federal takeover of the economy through measures such as the National Industrial Recovery Act and the creation of the Agriculture Adjustment Administration. In Roosevelt's first year in office, some forty new administrative agencies, referred to by historians as the alphabet soup agencies, were formed, shifting power away from Congress to expert administrators in the executive branch. An important and lasting example is the creation of the Securities and Exchange Commission in 1933, although similar expansions of federal power were accomplished in labor, trade, commerce, transportation, and other fields. As political scientist and historian Ira Katznelson pointed out, these were not merely new policies; instead, they "retrofit[ted] capitalism and shaped a welfare state."[24] Notably Roosevelt accomplished his major expansion of federal power without using tools intended for broad reforms: there were no constitutional amendments and no new cabinet offices created.

Herbert Hoover saw all this government planning and regulation of the economy and business as a form of "regimentation" that, rather than expanding equality of opportunity, actually restricted it. What is at stake in the New Deal, Hoover wrote in his 1934 book *The Challenge to Liberty*, is "the issue of human liberty."[25] While acknowledging imperfections in the American system, Hoover believed the system need not be undone, as Roosevelt proposed to do. Instead of liberty and freedom for the individual, Roosevelt promised national planning and regimentation carried out by the ever more powerful executive branch.[26] Hoover rightly feared that the "emergency acts" of the New Deal could become permanent.[27] By refocusing domestic policy on the forgotten man, the 25 percent who were less fortunate, Hoover argued that Roosevelt was harming "the 75 percent [who] need consideration also." "Through them," Hoover said, "is the sole hope for the 25 percent. If they be harassed, coerced, intimidated, discouraged, unduly taxed, the whole fabric will fall."[28]

To Roosevelt, on the other hand, political and legal equality of opportunity were not sufficient so long as people were unequal economically and socially. With industrialization and great concentrations of corporate economic power, it was time for the federal government to exercise its power in the economic realm. National planning, along with regulation of business, were the places to start, with greater attention to a fair distribution of wealth the ultimate goal. Historian David Kennedy described Roosevelt's goal as establishing "a new economic constitutional order."[29]

The notion that equality of opportunity was, for Roosevelt, a question of economic and social equality was foreshadowed in his Commonwealth Club speech and became increasingly clear as his administration progressed. In his second inaugural address on January 20, 1937, for example, Roosevelt maintained that "as intricacies of human relationships increase, so power to govern them also must increase." That meant more than escaping a depression, as Roosevelt pivoted to "a new order of things." Pointing to the "one-third of a nation ill-housed, ill-clad, ill-nourished," Roosevelt said that going forward, "The test of our progress is not whether we add more to the abundance of those who have much; it is whether we provide enough for those who have too little."

Roosevelt began to describe his larger equality of opportunity agenda in terms of providing government security for everyone. Instead of the self-reliance and rugged individualism of old, Roosevelt sought a government that would protect people against uncertainty, including the vagaries of the market. His "four freedoms speech" of January 6, 1941, included not only the First Amendment protections of freedom of speech and worship, but also his own platform of freedom from want and fear. In Roosevelt's 1944 State of the Union message, he documented a growing list of social and economic rights that Americans should enjoy, including the rights to a useful and remunerative job; earnings to provide adequate food, clothing, and recreation; a decent home; medical care; education; and protection from fears of old age, sickness, accident, and unemployment. Indeed, as Eric Rauchway has argued in his new book *Winter War*, Roosevelt ultimately embraced the Progressive dream and became a "social justice warrior," advocating for guarantees of jobs, unemployment insurance, old-age protections, and a broad course of "lasting improvement to the ordinary institutions of American life."[30]

Conclusion: A Turning Point in Equality of Opportunity

One useful approach to tracing the history of equality of opportunity is by locating turning points when the meaning of the term underwent fundamental change, and the New Deal provided one of those moments. Herbert Hoover essentially articulated the Founders' view of the term, that America was a land in which individuals were equally free to pursue happiness each in his or her own way. Having abandoned the class systems of Europe, Americans were born equal and the Constitution protected that equality. After slavery was eliminated, they enjoyed the fair chance of Abraham Lincoln, able to run the race of life from an equal starting point. Equality of opportunity was a companion piece to American individualism, enabling it here, softening any harshness there.

Since the late nineteenth century, however, Progressives had been building their case that equality of opportunity was a myth. They reluctantly admitted that it might have worked for a while on the American frontier but, with industrialization and economic collapse, it was well and truly over. It was time, as the Progressive president Teddy Roosevelt had argued, for the national government to step in and establish a Square Deal, which would deliver equality of opportunity to all the American people. This, the Progressives argued, meant economic and social fairness broadly understood, not merely legal or constitutional fairness. And this was a power, according to Teddy Roosevelt, that the federal government possessed under the interstate commerce clause of the Constitution.

Finally, the Great Depression had provided an inflection point when such a radical change in the American understanding of equality of opportunity could be addressed and Franklin Roosevelt became the leader who would do so. Indeed, one might even argue that, by the end of his lengthy administration, FDR had changed the goal from equality of opportunity to economic security guaranteed by government for the American people. These essential questions about equality of opportunity were framed by the Hoover-Roosevelt debates and would continue to be addressed throughout the modern era of American politics.

Notes

1. Gordon Lloyd and David Davenport, *The New Deal and Modern American Conservatism: A Defining Rivalry* (Stanford, CA: Hoover Institution Press, 2014).

2. Gerald F. Seib, "In Crisis, Opportunity for Obama," *Wall Street Journal*, November 21, 2008.

3. David M. Kennedy, *Freedom from Fear: The American People in Depression and War, 1929–1945* (New York: Oxford University Press, 1999), 11.

4. See George H. Nash, ed., *The Crusade Years, 1933–35* (Stanford, CA: Hoover Institution Press, 2013); and also Lloyd and Davenport, *New Deal*.

5. American Rhetoric, "Top 100 Speeches," https://www.americanrhetoric.com /top100speechesall.html.

6. Kennedy, *Freedom from Fear*, 373.

7. Sidney M. Milkis and Jerome M. Mileur, eds., *The New Deal and the Triumph of Liberalism* (Amherst, MA: University of Massachusetts Press, 2002), 35.

8. Rexford G. Tugwell, "The Progressive Orthodoxy of Franklin D. Roosevelt," *Ethics* 64, no. 1 (October 1953): 259.

9. Adolf A. Berle and Gardiner C. Means, *The Modern Corporation and Private Property* (New York: Commerce Clearing House, 1932).

10. Tugwell, "Progressive Orthodoxy," 262.

11. Adolf A. Berle, "Memorandum to Governor Franklin D. Roosevelt, August 15, 1932," Berle Papers, box 15, "Memorandum from Campaign," Franklin D. Roosevelt Presidential Library & Museum, 1.

12. Tugwell, "Progressive Orthodoxy," 266.

13. Frederick Jackson Turner, *The Significance of the Frontier in American History*, State Historical Society of Wisconsin, 1894.

14. Alexis de Tocqueville, *Democracy in America*, ed. Harvey C. Mansfield and Delba Winthrop (Chicago: University of Chicago Press, 2000), vol. 1 of 2, part 1, chapter 3, "Social State of the Anglo-Americans."

15. Henry Steele Commager, "Farewell to Laissez-Faire," *Current History* 38 (August 1933): 513.

16. Harold L. Ickes, *The New Democracy* (New York: W.W. North & Company, 1934), 17, 19, 60.

17. Donald R. Brand, "Competition and the New Deal Regulatory State," in Milkis and Mileur, *New Deal*, 169.

18. Herbert Croly, *Progressive Democracy* (New York: The McMillan Company, 1915), 97–98.

19. Kennedy, *Freedom from Fear*, 374.

20. See David Davenport and Gordon Lloyd, *Rugged Individualism: Dead or Alive?* (Stanford, CA: Hoover Institution Press, 2017), 31–34.

21. Richard Norton Smith, *An Uncommon Man: The Triumph of Herbert Hoover* (New York: Simon & Schuster, 1984), 172.

22. Lloyd and Davenport, *New Deal*.

23. Nash, *Crusade Years*.

24. Ira Katznelson, *Fear Itself: The New Deal and the Origins of Our Time* (New York: Liveright, 2013), 238.

25. Herbert Hoover, *The Challenge to Liberty* (New York: Charles Scribner's Sons, 1934), 1.

26. Hoover, 111–12.

27. Hoover, 192.

28. Herbert Hoover, *Addresses upon the American Road 1933–38* (New York: Charles Scribner's Sons, 1938), 56.

29. Kennedy, *Freedom from Fear*, 374.

30. Eric Rauchway, *Winter War* (New York: Basic Books, 2018), 143, 151.

CHAPTER THREE

The Great Society and Equality of Opportunity

A Revolution in Thinking and Policy Making

If Franklin Roosevelt and his New Deal of the 1930s paved the way for a revolution in equality of opportunity, Lyndon Johnson and his Great Society meant to carry it out in the 1960s. One might say that FDR was John the Baptist, the prophet heralding and laying out the path for a major change, and LBJ sought to be the savior bringing it to fruition. Roosevelt inaugurated the pathbreaking Social Security program, but Johnson would lead the Eighty-Ninth Congress to implement a host of civil rights and welfare measures that transformed government's role in the equality realm.

Lyndon Johnson considered himself a disciple of Franklin Roosevelt. He served as one of the president's young leaders in Congress and told an aide the day following John F. Kennedy's assassination: "I am a Roosevelt New Dealer."[1] Yet, Johnson was a different man whose presidency occurred in a different time. As a boy, Johnson lived a hardscrabble life in rural Texas and knew poverty firsthand. As a young schoolteacher, he was shaped by the difficult lives of his impoverished Mexican American students. His primary job experience before becoming president was serving in the Congress, especially as the powerful majority leader of the US Senate. Consequently, Johnson came into the presidency with a passion to ameliorate poverty and inequality and with a mastery of the levers of power to take action.

Just as Johnson's upbringing and experience were far different from those of that wealthy son of the Eastern establishment, Franklin Roosevelt, so too were the times in which he served as president. In the 1930s Roosevelt was responsible for guiding the country through a worldwide depression of unprecedented proportion. To the extent his New Deal effected major long-term changes in governance—and it surely did—they were generated from, and to some degree limited by, a major crisis. Roosevelt's argument was to change America in ways that would take care of people affected by the calamity and make sure that the federal government's expanded powers would prevent anything similar in the future.

By contrast, Americans in the 1960s, when LBJ became president, were living in an economic boom. Wealth and affluence were accompanied by a kind of conceit that America had mastered the economy and could now plan for the world it wanted to shape indefinitely. Johnson came to describe that world as "the Great Society." Amity Shlaes, in her book on the Great Society, compared the world of the 1960s to a popular television program of the time, *Bonanza*, in which the cowboy characters had outgrown the hardships of the western frontier and were busy trying to take care of the economic plenty that had fallen to them.[2]

While Roosevelt had responded to the need for economic and social security for the American people, Johnson was free to dream up and build a Great Society. In his first year alone, he declared war on poverty, secured the votes for national health insurance for retirees (Medicare) in 1965, and signed the first general federal aid to education law. Historian Arthur Schlesinger, who had served as President John Kennedy's advisor, wrote that it was time for liberals to quit worrying over the economic basics of life, which was a battle that had been won, and instead to "move on to the more subtle and complicated problem of fighting for individual dignity, identity and fulfillment in a mass society."[3] This is what Lyndon Johnson intended to do.

An important part of the unfolding story of equality of opportunity is how Roosevelt's understanding of the term and Johnson's intentions for it differed. Roosevelt believed that the traditional American understanding of equality of opportunity was no longer operative, with the western frontier now conquered and an agrarian economy replaced by industrialization. Now the government needed to step in to regulate and manage the economy and guarantee equality of opportunity to all.

Johnson believed that Roosevelt's broad approach had not worked for the lower classes of America, and especially for Black Americans. He was, therefore, prepared to undertake a major government initiative specifically aimed at certain groups of people in an effort to bring them into the equality narrative. Government under both Roosevelt and Johnson moved from guaranteeing legal equality to guaranteeing economic and social equality but, whereas previous understandings of equality of opportunity sought to ignore class and race, Johnson would specifically target poor Americans and Blacks in his programs.

Johnson and the Rhetoric of Equality of Opportunity

One of the best ways to study Lyndon Johnson's approach to equality of opportunity is to review several of his speeches that addressed the topic. Less than two months into his unexpected presidency, he delivered his first State of the Union message to Congress on January 8, 1964. Johnson used the occasion to launch his War on Poverty and, in so doing, gave a clear road map to his views on welfare and equality of opportunity.

The War on Poverty itself came together very quickly. LBJ understood that he should make the completion of President John Kennedy's agenda a top legislative priority, but he also wanted a signature initiative that would be his own. He gathered his advisors at his Texas ranch in December of 1963, asking them to advise him on how to do something about poverty. Not much was known at the time about antipoverty policy and their recommendation was to undertake several pilot projects to scope out the problem. Not one given to small pilot projects, Johnson told them he would find $500 million in the budget for it and challenged them to figure out how to use it.

Only weeks later, Johnson stood before Congress and declared "an unconditional war on poverty." His stated objective was to help "one-fifth of all American families with incomes too small to even meet their basic needs." He promised to pursue poverty wherever it had taken root, with a goal of not just relieving it but "to cure it and, above all, to prevent it." Like other domestic wars on crime, drugs, terror, and so on, Johnson's War on Poverty is still being waged today.[4]

Johnson wanted to make it clear, however, that the War on Poverty was not to be won by simply giving money to those whose incomes were inadequate, but by creating opportunity for them. In the same State of the Union speech, as he discussed the several programs he would advocate, he underscored that "all of these increased opportunities . . . must be open to Americans of every color." Indeed, he said the goal of the antipoverty effort was specifically "to replace . . . despair with opportunity," with employment and education at the center of the effort. When he signed the Economic Opportunity Act later in the year, he said it did not represent "a handout or a dole" because "we learned long ago that answer is no answer. . . . The answer is opportunity." He told his economic advisor, Lester Thurow, "to remove from the text of the [War on Poverty] bill any portion that could be viewed as a cash support program—the emphasis was to be on *opportunity* not *entitlement*."[5] Right from the start of his administration, beginning with his signature War on Poverty initiative, the emphasis was on government programs to create and provide equality of opportunity primarily through education, job training, and employment.

The speech for which LBJ is best known is his "Great Society" commencement address delivered at the University of Michigan on May 22, 1964. Given that Franklin Roosevelt had his signature New Deal and Harry Truman had his Fair Deal, Johnson sought a mantra by which his administration would be identified. He first used the phrase *Great Society* in a speech at Ohio University on May 7, 1964, but employed it ten times in his University of Michigan message.[6] Johnson's speechwriter, Richard Goodwin, has said that his mandate for this address was "not to produce a catalogue of specific projects, but a concept, an assertion of purpose, a vision . . . that went beyond the liberal tradition of the New Deal."[7]

The Michigan speech describes a utopia that a rich and fully developed society might aspire to. Johnson began by setting as his theme the pursuit of happiness of the American people, calling this "the test of our success as a nation." He sought not just a "rich and powerful" society but also a great one. The Great Society, he continued, "demands an end to poverty and racial injustice," but Johnson said that was "just the beginning." It concerned everything from education to leisure, from beauty and nature to loneliness and isolation. It would be pursued, Johnson continued, in three places: in the cities, in the countryside, and in the classrooms of America.

Johnson's solution was built around a new "creative federalism," one that called upon both Washington and local governments. A close reading suggests that, if not explicitly, Johnson was implicitly expanding his theme of equality of opportunity. He called his program a "battle to give every citizen the full equality which God enjoins and the law requires," demanding "an end to poverty and racial injustice." He placed great emphasis on education, noting that one-fourth of Americans were not completing high school. "Learning," he said, "must offer an escape from poverty." Again, there is nothing about welfare or cash payments to people, but a lot about lending a helping hand to those unable to achieve the American dream.

A year later, however, at a commencement address at Howard University on June 4, 1965, Johnson addressed equality of opportunity in detail and, in the view of some, shifted his position. Although he had earlier declined the invitation to speak at this historically Black university, he accepted late in the day, perhaps having in mind the need to stem a building racial storm in America's cities.[8] In this speech, he underscored his support for equality of opportunity but then added that mere legal equality was not sufficient. "It is not enough just to open the gates of opportunity," Johnson said, continuing, "our citizens must have the ability to walk through those gates." He proposed that the next stage of "the battle for civil rights" must include "not just equality as a right and a theory but equality as a fact and equality as a result."

In this speech, Johnson also focused closely on "the American Negro" and the special problems of poverty in that community. He said that for "20 million Negroes . . . equality of opportunity is essential, but not enough, not enough." They faced two special problems, he said: poverty and the legacy of slavery. He acknowledged that Black poverty raised complex questions, including the family structure, that were not fully understood, but that these issues needed to be studied and addressed. Johnson did not specify what he meant when he said equality of opportunity was not enough; nor did he say specifically, as some have claimed, that he was prepared to move on to a stronger principle of equality of outcome or results. Suffice it to say for now that, however one interprets it, this speech articulated a different emphasis and constituted a turning point in Lyndon Johnson's approach to equality of opportunity.

Johnson delivered other speeches that touched on equality of opportunity. As Vice President, he spoke at Gettysburg on Memorial Day, 1963, proclaiming, "One hundred years ago the slave was freed. One hundred years later the Negro remains in bondage to the color of his skin." Identifying himself with Abraham Lincoln, the Great Emancipator, Johnson went on to say that "until opportunity is unconcerned with the color of men's skins, emancipation will be a proclamation but not a fact." It seemed evident even then that if something beyond the standard of legal equality of opportunity might be sought, it would be for Black Americans. Then, in remarks when he signed the Civil Rights Act on July 2, 1964, Johnson introduced a new phrase that might describe that something extra, calling for "equal treatment."

Equality of opportunity, then, was clearly key to Lyndon Johnson's approach. From his first State of the Union message, he was not interested in welfare and handouts but rather a hand up through education and jobs. However, as America's cities began to burn in race riots, Johnson articulated something more, admitting that equality of opportunity was not sufficient, especially for African Americans. He called for equality of opportunity as not just a theory or legal promise but as a "result," later pledging "equal treatment." In the section below on dilemmas, we will explore further what all this might mean.

LBJ and the Eighty-Ninth Congress: The Legislative Push

Lyndon Johnson came to the presidency as a master of the legislative process. Johnson's chief biographer, Robert Caro, aptly titled one of his volumes *Master of the Senate*. Presidential advisor Jack Valenti observed that Johnson "was a creature of Congress, a legislator by character and long experience, who was determined to push through a transformative body of laws that would constitute nothing less than a second New Deal."[9] Historian William Leuchtenberg reported that in an interview with the president in September 1965, Johnson said he "wanted to be recognized as the greatest presidential legislator in U.S. history."[10] With a strong support following President Kennedy's death, a large mandate from his sweeping win in the 1964 election, and his party's control of both houses of Congress, Johnson had sufficient wind at his back to enact his ambitious legislative program.

And legislate Johnson did. Under his leadership, the Eighty-Ninth Congress, seated from January 1965 to January 1967, passed nearly two hundred major bills. Johnson dubbed it "the Fabulous Eighty-ninth Congress."[11] Political scientist Martin J. Medhurst reported that the president and his majorities in Congress "would pass more social legislation between 1964 and 1968 than any other single administration in American history."[12]

Johnson chose to make federal aid to education his first, and he would say his most important, legislative initiative. Education had been his own path out of poverty and he believed it could "interrupt the cycle of poverty" for others.[13] He had what his biographer Robert Dallek called "an almost mystical faith in the capacity of education to transform people's lives and improve their standard of living."[14] Education was clearly a long-term investment in curing poverty and, therefore, goes on the Johnson ledger as an opportunity program, not a welfare initiative.

Federal support for and involvement in K–12 education is so routine today that it might be surprising that, prior to Johnson's Elementary and Secondary Education Act in 1965, there had been little federal role. Even then, the bill was largely a matter of spending more federal money, although his 1964 presidential opponent Barry Goldwater argued that with federal spending comes federal control. Federal spending for K–12 education in 1964, the year before this legislation was enacted, was $1.1 billion, and twenty years later it had ballooned to $19 billion.[15] Johnson added Head Start for preschool education and also federal support for higher education, expanding the federal role in what had once been a state and local matter. Despite heavy spending and new programs, it turned out that a direct link between increased educational expenditures and economic attainment drawing people out of poverty was difficult to establish.[16]

Similar investments in job training and increasing labor force participation sought to develop greater opportunity and thereby erase poverty. Emulating his mentor, Franklin Roosevelt, Johnson created a Job Corps to assist one hundred thousand disadvantaged men, half working on conservation projects and half receiving job training. He also assisted state and local governments in creating job training programs for an additional two hundred thousand people. In addition to their basis in antipoverty goals, these programs also responded to a report of the President's Commission on Juvenile Delinquency and Youth Crime during the Kennedy administration, concluding that the best way to control delinquency was "by building new opportunities for under privileged young people to find a useful place in the mainstream."[17] This approach came to be known as "opportunity theory."[18]

As noted previously, the War on Poverty and its signature legislation, the Economic Opportunity Act, was all about long-term opportunity rather than immediate welfare relief. Although the New Left would soon seek a shift to entitlement and welfare, as historian Gareth Davies observed, the Economic Opportunity Act remained consistent with America's deep-seated individualism, by which Lyndon Johnson felt constrained. It promised "a hand up, not a handout," celebrating American values and reaffirming "the nation's belief in equality of opportunity."[19]

The Rise of the Federal Role

By most any account, Lyndon Johnson's Great Society dramatically grew the federal role in addressing equality of opportunity as well as other economic and social policies. Prior to the 1960s, despite the New Deal, these matters had been seen as societal and not governmental in nature. As Nicholas Eberstadt noted in his review of the Great Society fifty years after its appearance, "The United

States in the early 1960s was not yet a modern welfare state: our only nation-wide social program . . . was the Social Security System."[20] Issues such as poverty, inequality, and discrimination were not thought to be questions for the government to tackle, but all that changed under Lyndon Johnson.[21]

One way the change has been described is that America learned to look to Washington, DC, for answers and solutions. A young staffer in the Franklin Roosevelt administration described what he called "our preoccupation with persuading people to look to Washington for the solution of problems and our sense of what a great change in public attitudes this involved."[22] Lyndon Johnson's expansive understanding of what government could and should do, along with the dynamic legislative record of the Great Society's early years, certainly reinforced this view. Historians describe this period as one in which "the public's faith in the unbounded capacity of their government to solve large, vexing problems like poverty and disease" grew, in the process teaching Americans "to expect more from government."[23] Even if the problems of the Great Society years persist, so too do many of its policies and structures, including the war on poverty that continues.

Political scientist James Q. Wilson had a different way of expressing how the Great Society changed the role of the federal government. According to Wilson, the Great Society lowered "the legitimacy barrier for federal action."[24] Whereas before there had been debates over whether the federal government had the constitutional power to act in domestic matters such as welfare or education, Wilson said those questions about the legitimacy of federal action were resolved by Johnson and "political conflict takes a very different form. New programs need not await the advent of a crisis or an extraordinary majority because no program is any longer 'new'—it is seen, rather, as an extension, a modification, or an enlargement of something the government is already doing."[25] This was certainly the case with equality of opportunity and welfare, for example, as succeeding presidents such as Richard Nixon, Gerald Ford, and Jimmy Carter largely followed and even expanded the Great Society legacy and programs.

Once a societal goal referenced in the Declaration of Independence and protected by the Constitution, equality of opportunity had now become a

government program. Its meaning had shifted from giving all men and women
the freedom to pursue opportunities to the government's providing funding
to certain groups of people in order to assure they had opportunities. Equality
of opportunity was no longer a matter of legal guarantees and moral practices
but rather a question of social and economic policy directed by the federal
government. This was a journey begun during Franklin Roosevelt's New Deal
but brought to fruition in Lyndon Johnson's Great Society. Johnson said it in
speeches and passed a number of laws, growing the federal role. But with that
grew dilemmas and challenges.

Pursuing Equality in a Culture of Individualism

Public policy is faced with both problems to be solved and, at a somewhat
deeper level, dilemmas to be managed. A problem is an obstacle of some sort
between Point A, where we are now, and Point B, where we want to go. In these
cases, policy makers become problem solvers, charting a course over, around, or
through the problems—sometimes even blowing them up. Dilemmas, on the
other hand, are situations in which two or more values are present and we need
to preserve them both. They are not served by resolving them into black-or-
white, either-or choices. In the COVID-19 crisis, for example, did we want public health or a functioning economy? We needed both, so that was a dilemma to
be managed, not a problem subject to some final resolution.

In pursuing equality of opportunity, the Great Society confronted several
of these dilemmas, many of which continue to this day. One has been part of the
American republic since the Founding: the relationship between liberty and
equality. As Tocqueville observed in his *Democracy in America*, America was a
land of liberty but "what [Americans] love with a love that is eternal is equality."[26] But no sooner had the Declaration of Independence stated that all men
were "created equal" than it also affirmed their "inalienable" right to liberty and
the pursuit of happiness. As expressed in chapter 1, there is a deep tension between the two concepts, one that has played out through many chapters of our
nation's history, including the Great Society. In designing his equal opportunity

programs, therefore, Lyndon Johnson "would be swimming against a strong tide of individualism in American society, an ethos that prized self-reliance and condemned government largesse to the poor as counter productive."[27]

One of Lyndon Johnson's cabinet members, Secretary of Health, Education, and Welfare John Gardner, authored a book whose title—*Excellence: Can We Be Equal and Excellent Too?*— captured a related tension.[28] In it, he expresses his understanding that while the American people value individual freedom and choice, they also want all Americans to have equality, or at least equality of opportunity, calling liberty and equality the two souls in the breasts of most Americans.[29] Pursuing equal results or outcomes, Gardner acknowledged, tips the scale too far away from freedom and individualism. Gardner essentially concluded that Americans want as much equality as can be had within the context of a freedom-loving society that honors individualism. He described true equality of opportunity in that kind of society as an ideal, but not a reality.[30]

When Lyndon Johnson assumed the presidency in 1963, America was not a welfare state. Even Social Security had been described by President Franklin Roosevelt as a kind of insurance, or an investment that would be returned in people's senior years. With the country enjoying economic prosperity, there was no felt need to revolutionize the American economic system, so whatever Johnson wanted to accomplish about equality of opportunity needed to be done in the context of American individualism and liberty. While Americans might be persuaded to do something about poverty, for example, there was no appetite for large-scale redistribution of wealth or the creation of a welfare state. There was no need to worry about slicing the economic pie at a time when the pie was growing with seemingly enough for everyone to have a piece.

Equality of opportunity, then—providing a hand up, not a handout— became a wise political course, a way of managing the dilemma of helping the poor, especially the Black poor, without calling for a change to the American system of individualism and liberty. This had often been described as helping the "deserving" but not the "undeserving" poor—those who worked when they were able versus those who did not.[31] Political scientist George Klosko, in his book *The Transformation of American Liberalism*, argues that the Great

Society's antipoverty efforts were limited by the American culture of individualism, meaning that LBJ was able to pursue equality of opportunity but
not equality of results.[32] Klosko views this as a lost opportunity to transform
American liberalism into a true culture of "equality and human dignity that
are widely believed to underlie the welfare state."[33] As we shall see in the dis-
cussion of dilemma between equality of opportunity versus equality of results,
Johnson was able to push the liberal envelope, but not turn America into a
welfare state.

Equality of Opportunity Versus Equality of Results

An ongoing dilemma regarding equality of opportunity is whether it actually
is, or will inevitably become, equality of results. Is the relationship between the
two that they are two ends of a continuum, where a more freedom-loving and
individualistic culture believes in equality of opportunity and a welfare or so-
cialist state insists on equality of outcome? In other words, is the former more of
a pronouncement or aspiration with the latter a bottom line to be accomplished
no matter the cost? In that case, conservatives would generally favor the former
and liberals the latter. Another potential relationship between the two is that a
society continues to expand equality of opportunity so that, finally, it merges
into equality of outcome.

Historians have debated how the Great Society came down on the question
of equality of opportunity versus equality of results. Clearly, as described earlier,
Johnson's stated objective was equality of opportunity. He said he did not want
a dole or a welfare program; rather, he sought to open doors of opportunity.
His legislative emphasis was on education and jobs, both clearly long-term bets
on opportunity. Sargent Shriver, who headed Johnson's Office of Economic
Opportunity, understood the priority correctly, declaring, "Opportunity is our
middle name."[34] Labor Secretary Willard Wirtz, in a memorandum to the president, saw the priority as all-encompassing, writing, "A great deal of what you
want to do . . . could be effectively presented as a Program for Full Opportunity.
Having a chance is most of what life is about."[35]

The question is whether Johnson's commencement address at Howard University on June 4, 1965, represented a turning point away from equality of opportunity to something else—perhaps even to equality of results. Using the analogy of a race, in which equal opportunity gives each person a fair chance at the starting line, Johnson said: "You do not take a person who, for years, has been hobbled by chains and liberate him, bring him up to the starting line of a race and then say 'you are free to compete with all the others,' and still justly believe that you have been completely fair." No, said Johnson, "it is not enough just to open the gates of opportunity. All our citizens must have the ability to walk through those gates." Then came his powerful but perplexing answer to the dilemma: "This is the next and more profound stage of the battle for civil rights. We seek not just freedom but opportunity. We seek not just legal equity but human ability, not just equality as a right and a theory but equality as a fact and equality as a result."

In a single statement, Johnson said we seek "opportunity" but also "equality as a result." There are several ways to interpret this somewhat ambiguous statement. One understanding is that if equality of opportunity truly existed, you should see it in the results and, at least for Blacks, the results were not good. A somewhat stronger way to interpret it would be that once government achieved legal equality of opportunity, it was time to move on to other expressions of it, primarily in economic and social policy terms. According to this kind of thinking, government should not only guarantee equality of opportunity but also equality of the conditions necessary to take up those opportunities. Or, as LBJ put it, the government needs to help people without equal opportunities develop the "ability to walk through those gates."

Once the Voting Rights Act and other civil rights measures had guaranteed legal equality, the government, by this thinking, should turn to issues such as housing, neighborhoods, families, and other matters that affected equality of opportunity. As Nicholas Eberstadt noted in his fiftieth-year assessment of the Great Society, although we had ended legal discrimination, there were still "social, economic and attitudinal" problems limiting the advancement of Blacks, especially.

Amity Shlaes has argued that Lyndon Johnson's Howard University speech marked a significant shift in his own thinking. Having emphasized equality of opportunity in previous messages, Johnson in this speech "was institutionalizing a right to results," Shlaes claimed.[36] He now, according to Shlaes, had shared "his insistence that the nation go beyond equality of opportunity and pursue equality of result."[37] Theodore H. White agreed that LBJ's civil rights and poverty legislation amounted to "a substantial change" from "the quest for equality of opportunity to equality of result."[38] Although Johnson was now looking for results, and unable to find any that satisfied him, it is a strong assertion by these historians that he had now changed American policy to one that focuses on equality of results. It might be argued just as vigorously that Johnson felt if equality of opportunity were working, one should be able to see that in outcomes; which is somewhat different from the notion that, in a single speech, he shifted the purpose of government policy to equality of results.

Rhetorical scholar David Zarefsky has advanced a somewhat different view, maintaining that Lyndon Johnson effectively changed the meaning of equality of opportunity in the Howard speech.[39] Historically, equality of opportunity meant that law and government policy did not favor any group, allowing instead for individual opportunity, but now Johnson maintained that equality of opportunity required government action on behalf of certain groups.[40] As Zarefsky put it: "Government intervention in the 'opportunity structure,' once *forbidden*, is now *mandated*."[41] This was accomplished rhetorically, Zarefsky claims, by understanding that older notions of equality of opportunity only gave the "appearance of equal opportunity" but now government action was needed to bring about actual opportunity.[42] By this reasoning, Johnson did not really change the goal, but did change the meaning of terms.

Another scholarly view about Johnson's understanding of equality of opportunity and the Howard speech was advanced in a book by George Klosko. Klosko argues that Johnson had come to believe that something more than legal equality of opportunity was required and that what he asserted, beginning especially in the Howard speech, is "basic access" for all, an "equal ability to walk through the gates, without further regard to anything beyond ability to attain an acceptable level of achievement."[43] Klosko argues that Johnson might have sought a more radical advance, moving toward a welfare state, but he did not, settling for basic access, which "does not require equal distribution, [but] it does establish a level of resources necessary to allow people to pursue their opportunities with some prospect of advancement."[44] To put it succinctly, Klosko's notion of basic access entails "that people get what they need in order to have a shot."[45]

To summarize, it does seem evident that, beginning with the Howard speech, Johnson intended something more than what equality of opportunity had meant historically. It was to be more than a mere constitutional guarantee or a legal removal of obstacles. It would require government to become active in helping poor people, and especially poor Blacks, be better prepared to go through the gates of opportunity. As his biographer, Doris Kearns, said, "Johnson seemed to mean something more than equality of opportunity, that no one should be deprived of the essentials of a decent life."[46] In so doing, he did put government even further in the equality driver's seat, pressing harder on the pedal of government aid and engagement. One way of understanding this approach was to say that government should make sure certain people were not blocked from opportunity by structural barriers such as lack of education, poverty, or racism.[47] To call this now equality of results seems too strong, but it changed and expanded the traditional understanding of equality of opportunity.

Curing Poverty or Creating Opportunity

When Lyndon Johnson declared an "unconditional war on poverty" in his first State of the Union message, he was breaking new ground. Little was known about the nature and causes of poverty and even less about what government might do to address it. Was it simply a question of money and the challenge of bringing people's incomes up to a minimal level? Or was it deeper and more complicated than that? Michael Harrington, in his influential 1962 book, *The Other America*, argued that poverty in America had become a way of life and needed to be tackled by policy makers at multiple levels. Harrington specifically called out "Negro poverty" imposed by White America, saying that even if "all the laws were framed to provide equal opportunity . . . there would still be a vast, silent, and automatic system directed against men and women of color."[48] Harrington called for radical action, a "crusade against this poverty in our midst,"[49] and "a transformation of some of the basic institutions of society."[50]

The more direct, and perhaps easier, way to tackle poverty would have been for the government to make direct monetary transfers to poor people, which was increasingly the approach of European countries in the 1960s and 1970s. However, LBJ, whether out of his own conviction or because he knew Americans would not accept it, spoke against "the dole" and rejected the welfare state. Sargent Shriver, who directed Johnson's War on Poverty from his Office of Economic Opportunity, said, "We are not handing out anything to anybody, except more opportunities."[51] Ironically, even the popular conservative economist Milton Friedman, in his classic book of the era *Capitalism and Freedom*, had proposed that the government provide people with a universal basic income through a negative income tax.[52] Rather than spend tax money on providing public housing—a contemporary form of paternalism—why not give the poor money directly? "If funds are to be used to help the poor, would they not be used more effectively by being given in cash rather than in kind?" Friedman asked.[53] Then, too, we should provide a tax exemption in the form of a "negative income tax," thereby avoiding paternalistic government while still providing government relief for poverty consistent with market forces and personal choice.[54]

Although Lyndon Johnson spoke of a war on poverty, his rhetoric and programs were not oriented toward the immediate outcome of eliminating poverty but rather toward the longer-term approach of providing opportunity. His programs concerned education, jobs training, and labor force participation so that the poor and disadvantaged could realize their opportunities. As Brookings economist Henry J. Aaron put it: "Most of the elements of the War on Poverty rested on the faith that the establishment of equal opportunity would eventually reduce poverty to a vestigial curiosity."[55]

From a policy perspective, it now seems a bit odd that LBJ would not pursue both immediate poverty relief as well as long-term opportunities, managing this dilemma through a both/and rather than an either/or approach. One could both raise the floor with relief for those with incomes below the poverty level and also raise the ceiling by helping create greater opportunities. Robert A. Levine addresses this difficult dilemma in his book *The Poor Ye Need Not Have With You*, arguing that Johnson and his policy makers never fully addressed, or perhaps even understood, the twin problems of poverty and unequal opportunity.[56] Levine describes ameliorating poverty as relatively easy, but eliminating inequality of opportunity, which he argues was largely caused by racial discrimination and segregation, as quite difficult. He concludes that the War on Poverty doubtless helped lift some out of poverty, but he doubts that it made much of a dent in its real goal—to create greater equality of opportunity.[57]

This debate about relieving poverty versus creating opportunity could be understood as an early chapter in the longer-term debate on America's approach to welfare. It is clear, however, whether for political reasons or out of deep conviction, Lyndon Johnson veered away from welfare and toward governmental assistance in creating opportunity. Rather than manage this dilemma between curing poverty and creating opportunity, Johnson chose one horn of it, pursuing equality of opportunity as he had broadened it.

The Dilemma of Special Preferences

In the historical development of equality of opportunity, the word *opportunity* has received more attention, perhaps, than the term *equality*. If so, Lyndon Johnson meant to change that. He sought to put more *equality* into equality of opportunity and many of his speeches and programs moved in that direction. Johnson felt that a time of economic growth was the ideal moment to make certain that all segments of society were experiencing an opportunity to advance.

For all Franklin Roosevelt's talk about helping the forgotten man and establishing equality for all, his actions on that front were more limited. Of course, the context of Roosevelt's presidency, the Great Depression, generated a lot of forgotten men and women, and so his efforts on their behalf were necessarily broad-based. His undertaking to secure greater economic security was thus targeted at a major segment of the population. Roosevelt's public works projects put a large number of Americans back to work, and his Social Security system was an investment and insurance program for all, not relief for some. As political scientist Norman J. Orenstein put it in comparing the Roosevelt and Johnson presidencies, Roosevelt was putting out a fire and Johnson was looking for a transformation.[58]

The essence of Johnson's revolution or transformation was his decision to target special help and new opportunities toward specific groups of people, not just for a large swath of the population. To Johnson, this was essential to establish real equality. The need to do this was at the heart of Harrington's *The Other America*. Harrington argued that Black poverty had become a way of life, that "mass unemployment has been replaced by class unemployment."[59] But if Blacks could vote and civil rights legislation had been enacted, this meant special attention to social and economic problems affecting Black poverty.[60] It meant adding references to race or ethnic origin to employment and educational forms where those had been deleted.[61] As Hoover Institution scholar Seymour Martin Lipset observed, Johnson's approach changed America from the pursuit of equal opportunity for individuals, as was voiced in the Declaration of Independence, to "equality of results for groups."[62]

As it turned out, it was not at all clear that government knew how to eliminate Black poverty, at least it proved incapable of doing so. Further, with the diversion of resources to the war in Vietnam, many social agendas began to take a back seat in Washington. By the end of Johnson's term as president, opposition to his Great Society programs had developed on opposite political fronts: the New Left and a revived conservatism. Ironically, Johnson's Great Society ended up with Americans looking more to Washington to solve problems but trusting it less.

Conclusion

Lyndon Johnson's Great Society was a high-water mark for equality of opportunity and the policies that defined it. While Johnson himself promoted equality as a top priority, he nevertheless operated within the opportunity context. Although some see him as instituting so many changes to opportunity policy that he could be described as moving away from opportunity to equality of outcomes or results, a better interpretation of the Great Society approach would be to say that Johnson redefined opportunity. Rather than understanding opportunity as something government would allow individuals to pursue, Johnson put government fully into the business of creating and regulating opportunity. Whereas prior understandings of opportunity sought to keep government from favoring any group, the Great Society's deep concern with poverty, and especially Black poverty, prompted government to favor groups that needed a boost to get to the opportunity starting line. All this constituted a real revolution in both thought and policy for the equality of opportunity doctrine.

Some, in what came to be called the New Left, wanted to see liberals abandon equality of opportunity altogether, shifting to equality of outcomes and creating a full-on welfare state. Greater long-term impact, however, came not from the left but from the right, as conservatives responded to the Great Society and its policies. Barry Goldwater, who opposed Johnson in the 1964 presidential election, was a kind of prophet in the wilderness, calling out the excesses of the Great Society. Goldwater, from the open country of the Arizona West, believed very much in equality but opposed the notion that it was the role of government to solve it. He said, "I am unalterably opposed to . . . discrimination, but I also know that government can provide no lasting solution. . . . The ultimate solution lies in the hearts of men."[63]

Near the close of that 1964 campaign, on October 27, 1964, Ronald Reagan delivered a televised speech that has become famous in political history: "A Time for Choosing." Reagan the spokesman was both more optimistic and telegenic than Goldwater the candidate. Reagan pointed out that, under Lyndon Johnson and his Democratic predecessors, government spending, taxes, and regulation had reached peacetime highs. He described these as creating a risk to freedom and presenting Americans with a fundamental choice: continue down the path toward greater government control or promote freedom and self-government. Equality of opportunity and the War on Poverty were Great

Society microcosms of excessive government regulation, spending, and control. This choice, as Reagan described it, would finally be placed more powerfully before voters in his own successful 1980 campaign for the presidency, and it would launch a conservative counterrevolution to Lyndon Johnson's Great Society.

Notes

1. Randall B. Woods, *Prisoners of Hope* (New York: Basic Books, 2016), 15.

2. Amity Shlaes, *Great Society: A New History* (New York: HarperCollins, 2019), 21–22.

3. Arthur Schlesinger, "The Future of Liberalism: The Challenge of Abundance," *The Reporter*, May 3, 1956, 10.

4. See David Davenport and Gordon Lloyd, *How Public Policy Became War* (Stanford, CA: Hoover Institution Press, 2019).

5. Sidney M. Milkis, "How Great Was the Great Society?" in *A Companion to Lyndon B. Johnson*, ed. Mitchell B. Lerner (Malden, MA: Blackwell Publishing Ltd., 2012), 480.

6. Ursula Hackett, "The Six Great Societies," *Presidential Studies Quarterly* 46, no. 2 (June 2016): 294. Johnson used the phrase fifty-three times in official presidential speeches, proclamations, and signing statements. 292–93.

7. Woods, *Prisoners*, 54.

8. Woods, 187.

9. Julian E. Zelizer, *The Fierce Urgency of Now* (New York: Penguin Books, 2015), 2.

10. Robert Dallek, *Flawed Giant* (New York: Oxford University Press, 1998), 231.

11. Joshua Zeitz, *Building the Great Society* (New York: Viking Press, 2018), 185.

12. Martin J. Medhurst, "LBJ, Reagan, and the American Dream: Competing Visions of Liberty," *Presidential Studies Quarterly* 46, no. 1 (March 2016): 101–2.

13. Zeitz, *Great Society*, 149.

14. Dallek, *Flawed Giant*, 195–96.

15. Gene I. Maeroff, "After 20 Years, Educational Programs Are a Solid Legacy of Great Society," *New York Times*, September 30, 1985.

16. Henry J. Aaron, *Politics and the Professors: The Great Society in Perspective* (Washington, DC: The Brookings Institution, 1978), chapter 3.

17. Woods, *Prisoners*, 61.

18. Woods, 61.

19. Gareth Davies, *From Opportunity to Entitlement: The Transformation and Decline of Great Society Liberalism* (Lawrence, KS: University of Kansas Press, 1966), 39.

20. Nicholas Eberstadt, *The Great Society at Fifty* (Washington, DC: American Entereprise Institute, 2014), 2.

21. Aaron, *Politics*, 16.

22. Hugh Heclo, "Sixties Civics," in *The Great Society and the High Tide of Liberalism*, ed. Sidney M. Milkis and Jerome M. Mileur (Boston: University of Massachusetts Press, 2005), 57.

23. See, respectively, Zeitz, *Great Society*, 188; foreword by Sidney M. Milkis and Jerome M. Mileur in Milkis and Mileur, *High Tide*, xvi.

24. James Q. Wilson, "American Politics, Then and Now," *Commentary* (February 1979): 41.

25. Wilson, 41.

26. Alexis de Tocqueville, *Democracy in America*, ed. Harvey C. Mansfield and Delba Winthrop (Chicago: University of Chicago Press, 2000), 52.

27. Woods, *Prisoners*, 63.

28. John W. Gardner, *Excellence: Can We Be Equal and Excellent Too?* (New York: W. W. Norton & Co., 1984).

29. Gardner, 18.

30. Gardner, 106.

31. Davies, *From Opportunity to Entitlement*, 40.

32. George Klosko, *The Transformation of American Liberalism* (New York: Oxford University Press, 2017), 185.

33. Klosko, 249.

34. Klosko, 182.

35. David Zarefsky, *Political Argumentation in the United States* (Philadelphia: John Benjamins Publishing Co., 2014), 332.

36. Shlaes, *Great Society*, 167.

37. Shlaes, 206.

38. Theodore H. White, "Summing Up," *New York Times Magazine*, April 25, 1982, 32.

39. Zarefsky, *Political Argumentation*, 323.

40. Zarefsky, 323.

41. Zarefsky, 325.

42. Zarefsky, 329.

43. Klosko, *American Liberalism*, 191.

44. Klosko, 253.

45. Klosko, 255.

46. Doris Kearns, *Lyndon Johnson and the American Dream* (New York: Harper & Row, 1976), 215–16.

47. Medhurst, "LBJ, Reagan, and the American Dream," 101.

48. Michael Harrington, *The Other America: Poverty in the United States* (New York: MacMillan, 1962), 63, 71.

49. Harrington, 167.

50. Harrington, 72.

51. Klosko, *American Liberalism*, 182.

52. Milton Friedman and Rose D. Friedman, *Capitalism and Freedom* (Chicago: University of Chicago Press, 1962), 191–92.

53. Friedman and Friedman, 178.

54. Friedman and Friedman, 192.

55. Aaron, *Politics*, 26.

56. Robert A. Levine, *The Poor Ye Need Not Have with You: Lessons from the War on Poverty* (Cambridge, MA: The MIT Press, 1970), 29, 89.

57. Levine, 39, 187, 242.

58. Karen Tumulty, "The Great Society at 50," *Washington Post*, May 14, 2014.

59. Harrington, *The Other America*, 28.

60. Aaron, *Politics*, 153.

61. Zarefsky, *Political Argumentation*, 324–25.

62. Seymour Martin Lipset, "Equal Chances versus Equal Results," *The Annals of the American Academy of Political and Social Science* 523, no. 1 (September 1, 1992): 64.

63. "Now the Vote," *New York Times*, November 1, 1964.

CHAPTER FOUR

The Reagan Counterrevolution

Lyndon Johnson's Great Society launched a new era of equality of opportunity. It had been left to individuals to locate opportunity, but now it became the job of the federal government to create it—especially for those living in poverty and for certain ethnic groups, primarily Blacks. The Great Society's high-profile War on Poverty was one key program designed to generate more opportunity, but there were many others in civil rights, housing, and job training. The Great Society transformed the federal government's role in welfare and, in so doing, came up with a new narrative for equality of opportunity.

Just as Dwight Eisenhower had disappointed conservatives by not turning back Franklin Roosevelt's sweeping New Deal programs, Richard Nixon, elected in 1968 to succeed Lyndon Johnson, largely continued and even expanded the Great Society initiatives. Nixon is famous for saying, of economics, "We're all Keynesians now," but equally he seemed to accept that we all lived in the Great Society welfare state now.

Nixon increased spending in a number of Great Society programs during his first term, including larger expenditures for food stamps and school lunches and the addition of two million more people to the Medicare rolls. In addition to increasing Social Security benefits, Nixon tied payments automatically to the rate of inflation. Historian Julian Zelizer summarized these increases to the several Great Society programs when he wrote that federal expenditures for Americans living in poverty increased 50 percent between 1969 and 1973.[1] By the time Gerald Ford became president in 1974, Zelizer noted, "Great Society programs had become even more severely entrenched politically."[2]

Although many assume that affirmative action and quotas in hiring came during the Great Society, Nixon was actually responsible for those expansions of equality programs. Historian Dean J. Kotlowski, in his article "Richard Nixon and the Origins of Affirmative Action," confirms that Nixon was the one "who first sanctioned formal goals and time frames," thereby formalizing what came to be called affirmative action.[3] Nixon's Philadelphia Plan required construction companies to establish and meet minority hiring goals, a form of quota established privately, not by the government. It is often said that, as *Fortune* magazine declared: "It was the Nixonites who gave us employment quotas."[4]

This continues a pattern of Republican presidents accepting and maintaining the expansionist government policies of their Democratic predecessors. Notably, Eisenhower continued Franklin Roosevelt's New Deal programs and, after several Republican presidents, they remain today. William F. Buckley referred to this "easy and wholehearted acceptance" of "the great statist legacy of the New Deal" as one of "measured socialism."[5] As Nixon advisor Pat Buchanan noted, Nixon, too, decided to leave Johnson's Great Society programs largely in place, accepting them as the new status quo.[6] Perhaps leaving things as they are—as Nixon did, leaving equality of opportunity as a government program— rather than rolling back major Washington programs is itself a form of conservatism. Or, the kind of increased federal aid programs instituted by Roosevelt and Johnson may simply have become too popular to challenge later. In any event, both the New Deal and Great Society had established a new normal by the time Ronald Reagan took office in 1981.

Lost Confidence in Government Programs

While new leaders had largely accepted prior government programs, by the late 1970s the people were losing confidence in government's ability to solve problems, leading to a worldwide conservative counterrevolution to Great Society liberalism. Besides Ronald Reagan's electoral win in 1980, in Britain Margaret Thatcher led her Conservative Party to victory in 1979, while in Canada Brian Mulroney pushed out the liberal Pierre Trudeau in 1984. Martin Anderson, Reagan's domestic policy advisor, noted in his book *Revolution* that there were similar conservative turns in other countries as well.[7]

Whereas the Great Society had been advanced during a robust economy in the 1960s, the 1970s were a very different time economically. If the 1960s were a time of affluence and steady economic growth, the 1970s were marked by Richard Nixon's imposition of wage and price controls, Gerald Ford's WIN (Whip Inflation Now) campaign, and Jimmy Carter's trifecta of high inflation, high interest rates, and high unemployment. If the 1960s were a time of economic security, the 1970s were characterized by fear and insecurity. Political scientist Mark A. Smith noted a steady decline in economic security beginning in 1973, continuing through the Carter years to the end of the decade.[8] Smith observed that Republicans wisely began to focus their rhetoric and policies on the economy in the 1970s, creating political opportunities.

Then, too, there was a growing recognition that the sweeping Great Society programs had not performed as expected, that poverty, inequality, racism, and other problems were still alive and well despite new government efforts and increased federal spending. Just as we thought in the 1960s that we had figured out how to keep the economy stable and growing, we had come to believe government could solve even bigger problems, such as poverty. As Peter Schrag wrote in 1970, however, "We thought we had solutions to everything—poverty, racism, injustice, ignorance; it was supposed to be only a matter of time, of money, of proper programs, of massive assaults. . . . It is now clear that the confidence is gone, that many of the things we *knew* no longer seem sure or even probable."[9]

Charles Murray's landmark book *Losing Ground* vividly captured the failure of the federal government's antipoverty and welfare programs.[10] Although not without controversy, Murray nevertheless documented how much the federal government undertook and spent compared with how little outcome was produced. For example, Murray pointed out, "In 1968, as Lyndon Johnson left office, 13 percent of Americans were poor, using the official definition. Over the next twelve years, our expenditures on social welfare quadrupled. And, in 1980, the percentage of poor Americans was—13 percent."[11]

At the time LBJ launched his War on Poverty, very little was known about antipoverty programs. Because of so little experience or knowledge in the field, Johnson's advisors had recommended a series of smaller pilot programs to see what worked. Johnson, however, was no small-program politician and, instead, he launched a vague but extensive War on Poverty. This was not just an effort to put more money into the pockets of poor people, but rather an attempt to address the problem of "structural poverty." This was the population described in Michael Harrington's *The Other America*, which argued that a million people were living in our midst invisibly but nevertheless in poverty, especially racial minorities, the unskilled, the aged, women heading households, and so on.[12]

It turned out that structural poverty was far more difficult to reach and correct than anyone expected. As Murray pointed out, despite job-training programs, the employment rate for young black males—a key component in addressing structural poverty—went down dramatically.[13] Although the poverty rate dipped some in the late 1960s—hardly the result of small and new programs of the day—it inexplicably "skyrocketed in the 70s."[14] Ronald Reagan would later quip, "Some years ago, the federal government declared war on poverty, and poverty won."

In his book arguing that Franklin Roosevelt and Ronald Reagan were transformative, bookend presidents of the twentieth century, author John W. Sloan concluded, "By the 1970s, New Deal liberalism was largely a spent force."[15] Whereas the robust economy of the 1960s had fueled government expansion and new programs, it was clear by the 1970s that a new economic model was needed. Clearly, by the time of the Reagan-Carter election in 1980, with long lines and rationing at gas stations, double-digit inflation and interest rates, along with high unemployment, the people were ready for a change and, in the 1980 presidential election, they voted for one.

Building Toward a Conservative Counterrevolution

A number of philosophical and political initiatives over at least five decades culminated in the election of Ronald Reagan as a conservative president in

1980. Although conventional wisdom credits the birth of modern American conservatism to Russell Kirk, William F. Buckley's *National Review*, and other conservative thinkers in the 1950s, we have argued that Herbert Hoover, in his response to what he saw as the excesses of the New Deal in the 1930s, was actually the prophet who called forth the basic ideas of contemporary conservatism.

In our book *The New Deal and Modern American Conservatism: A Defining Rivalry*, we made the case that Franklin Roosevelt's New Deal was effectively America's French Revolution, changing everything.[16] Indeed, it is still the paradigm for domestic and economic policy today, as we simply add new government programs to its template. Herbert Hoover, who had previously been known as a kind of progressive Republican, was shocked by the expansive New Deal and began giving speeches and writing books that exposed its overreach.[17] In both our book and George Nash's *The Crusade Years*, we come to see a changed Herbert Hoover, one who had become a full-throated conservative in opposition to the New Deal.[18] We describe Hoover as a prophet in the wilderness, without much direct impact on public policy of the day, but nevertheless laying out the case for what has become modern American conservatism. In an earlier book, Gordon Lloyd further demonstrated how the Hoover-Roosevelt "debates" of the 1930s foreshadowed the clashes between liberals and conservatives today.[19]

Conservatism took another major step forward as a coherent political philosophy in the 1950s and 1960s, primarily through books and journals published by conservative thinkers. Russell Kirk's *The Conservative Mind*, published in 1953, made the case for a traditional Burkean conservatism in American politics. Friedrich Hayek's *The Road to Serfdom*, though published in the 1940s, received much attention in the 1950s for promoting the primacy of economic freedom. William F. Buckley's *God and Man at Yale* in 1951 drew attention to the importance of religion and values in the conservative philosophy. A bit later, James Burnham's *Suicide of the West* decried liberals' efforts to use government to cure every social evil. Milton Friedman emerged with an economic view of conservatism in his *Capitalism and Freedom*. These authors all represented various strains of conservatism that were under development and winning followers in the 1950s and 1960s.

The historian of modern American conservatism, George Nash, has observed that the movement "is not, and has never been, univocal. It is a *coalition* with many points of origin and diverse tendencies."[20] In the 1950s and 1960s, however, two things drew these several flavors of conservatism together: anticommunism, and the launch of the big conservative umbrella *National Review*. The former was really the glue that held conservatism together from the 1950s until the fall of the Berlin Wall in 1989. Buckley's *National Review* was a rare vehicle that, under the editorship of Frank Meyer, promoted "fusionism," or an embrace of all the elements and supporters of conservatism. As Nash summarized: fusionism triumphed through the work of Frank Meyer and *National Review* while anticommunism provided "cement." They embraced a "day-to-day conservatism they felt 'in their hips,'" a phrase used by Midwestern conservative author Willmore Kendall.[21]

Conservatism moved from the realm of thought and ideas into the political sphere with Senator Barry Goldwater's run for the presidency in 1964. As a Western conservative, Goldwater faced the challenge of uniting the Republican Party that had been dominated by liberals and moderates from the East. Then, having won the nomination, he had to take on an incumbent president, Lyndon Johnson, who was carrying out the legacy of a martyr, John F. Kennedy. Goldwater was more a man of principle than a politician and was successfully portrayed by the Democrats as an extremist—a label he embraced himself when he said in his convention acceptance speech, "extremism in the defense of liberty is no vice." Beating LBJ would have been a tall order for any Republican, perhaps most of all Goldwater. Still, conservatism had come to the fore as a national political force, and many conservatives had taken grassroots positions within the Republican Party. The conservatives would be heard from again.

Ronald Reagan and "A Time for Choosing"

One important development late in the Goldwater campaign was a televised speech by a former actor and corporate motivational speaker, Ronald Reagan. Following his career in Hollywood, in which he had been a union leader and a Democrat, Reagan had gone to work for General Electric delivering "The Speech," as it was known, at company facilities around the country. As Reagan worked in this corporate environment, and followed GE's mandate to create "a better business climate," he began to see more clearly how government affected business and a newfound conservatism began to take root in his thinking.[22] Before leading a national political counterrevolution, Reagan had first experienced his own personal political transformation.

On October 27, 1964, Reagan delivered "The Speech" on national television on behalf of Barry Goldwater's presidential campaign. Although it was too little, too late to secure a victory for Goldwater, the speech effectively launched Reagan's own political career. Indeed, "A Time for Choosing," as it has become known, is considered one of the great political speeches in recent American history. Since it lays out Reagan's view of Lyndon Johnson's Great Society and of his own conservative ideas, this address deserves further attention.

Lyndon Johnson actually set the stage for the "choosing" theme in his own acceptance speech at the Democratic National Convention on August 27, 1964. In that address he said, "We do offer the people a choice, a choice of continuing on the courageous and compassionate course that has made this nation the strongest and freest and most prosperous and the most peaceful nation in the history of mankind." Johnson reiterated in a campaign speech on October 9, 1964, "You have your choice."

For Reagan, then, the 1964 campaign became "A Time for Choosing." The essential choice presented by Reagan was what the role, size, funding, and objectives of the federal government should be. Would it be expansive, as LBJ's Great Society proposed, or limited, as Barry Goldwater favored? Reagan made it clear that an expansive federal government was contrary to the views of the Founders, a "betrayal of the spirit of 1776," as he said in the speech. Part of the problem, as Reagan diagnosed it, was government's size, since "no government ever voluntarily reduces itself in size." The government achieves this in part by taking on new projects, such as its expanded role in the farm economy, in urban renewal, and a War on Poverty. The number of government workers, now "one out of six in the nation's work force," also demonstrated the excessive size

Reagan asserted. A related problem is the financial cost of government, with taxes then "37 cents out of every dollar earned," or "$17 million a day more than the government takes in."

Especially troubling to Reagan was the government planners who had been unleashed by the Great Society. These efforts were not only fruitless, he felt, but also meddlesome, constituting an incursion into the lives of Americans and limiting their individual freedom. He attacked President Johnson's assertion that we must accept "greater government activity in the affairs of the people." He singled out the role of the federal government in the farm economy, noting, "In the last three years we have spent $43 in feed grain programs for every bushel of corn we don't grow." He decried "the schemes of the do-gooders" who built an expensive and ineffectual welfare state. To Reagan, all this added up to trading "our freedom for the soup kitchen of the welfare state." Reagan concluded his speech by an appeal for individual freedom, noting, "Barry Goldwater has faith that you and I have the ability and the dignity and the right to make our own decisions and determine our own destiny."

In this speech that introduced Ronald Reagan to the political world, Reagan staked out the broad outlines of the conservative narrative of equality of opportunity. The conservative counterrevolution was aimed at reducing the intrusive role of the federal government in favor of an earlier understanding of equality of opportunity that emphasized individual freedom. The Great Society's equality programs, especially welfare and the War on Poverty, were ineffective and misguided and needed to be rolled back. People should pay fewer taxes and keep more of their own money. Reagan saw this as not only consistent with the limited role of government advocated by the Founders and laid out in the Constitution, but consistent with the core principle of keeping people free. This speech became a kind of road map for understanding the conservative counterrevolution.

Reagan contrasted the self-reliance of the Founding with the excessive spending of the Great Society. Our right to life, liberty, and property do not come from government, he warned. Reagan effectively argued that the Great Society was pushing change to the American tradition, offering disincentives to work.

The myth of the Great Society, according to Reagan, was that government—especially a large, ever-growing, costly, and absurdly run centralized federal government—can and should solve social problems such as poverty rather than allow individuals, communities, and the market system to solve the problem. Government entitlement programs are not only inefficient; they actually offer disincentives. Individual freedom is especially fragile up against a centralized government determined to do good by removing our own sense of personal responsibility to work and care for our own families. Of course, we must aid the needy, but we must not provide incentives for them to remain needy.

The Reagan Counterrevolution

Just as Lyndon Johnson and Franklin Roosevelt led equality revolutions during their presidencies, Ronald Reagan led a counterrevolution. Reagan's policies were informed by his conviction that opportunity was better provided by getting government out of the way of individual initiative than by government seeking to create opportunity through policies and programs. His desire was to let people pursue their own opportunity. Though he later spoke of creating an "opportunity society," Reagan espoused policies on equality of opportunity that were more a derivative of his larger goal—that of reducing the size and role of government. To identify and understand his equality of opportunity policies, then, we must also look at his larger approach to the size and role of the federal government, the need to lower taxes and reduce government regulation, and the importance of economic growth.

The first plank of Reagan's opportunity platform was to reduce the size and role of the federal government that he saw as interfering with individual freedom and opportunity. This became clear when he famously said, in his first inaugural address: "Government is not the solution to our problem, government is the problem." In a diary entry on August 5, 1982, Reagan wrote, "We saw and heard the impossible management structure of our government. It is by any standard a cumbersome, costly, incompetent monster."[23] Reagan described the consequence of too much government in a speech at Notre Dame on May 17, 1981, saying, "Central government has usurped powers" in ways that led to "misuses of power and preemption of the prerogatives of the people and their social institutions." Indeed, as the Republican platform of 1980 put it, "We seek to restore the family, the neighborhood, the community and the workplace as vital alternatives in our national life to ever-expanding federal power." Too much federal government, then, by Reagan's reckoning, pushed out opportunity rather than creating it. As he said in a radio address on May 5, 1984, we must get this "monster under control so we can have government of, by, and for the people, not the other way around."

The burgeoning growth of federal programs under Johnson, and their inability to solve problems, created an environment in which Reagan's contrarian case for less government could be heard and accepted. As Jonathan Darman put it in his book *Landslide: LBJ and Ronald Reagan at the Dawn of a New America*, "Johnson promised that his government would soon deliver the nation from all troubles, but the nation grew more troubled by the day. Only then did the conservative case against government begin to seem not so crazy after all."[24] In America's historic balance between individualism— where Reagan thought real opportunity lay—and government intervention, he clearly felt the Great Society had tipped the balance too far in the latter direction. Again, in his first inaugural address, he spoke of this as the need to "reverse the growth of government" and restore "the balance between the levels of government."

Notably, however, Reagan apparently thought of the Great Society as having altered the role of government far more, or more intrusively, than Franklin Roosevelt's New Deal. On January 28, 1982, Reagan wrote in his diary, "The press is dying to paint me as now trying to undo the New Deal. I remind them I voted for FDR 4 times. I'm trying to undo the 'Great Society.' It was LBJ's war on poverty that led to our present mess."[25] Although Reagan did not elaborate on the key differences between FDR and LBJ, others have noted that Roosevelt's agenda primarily concerned economic security, whereas Johnson's Great Society was more about government planning and the redistribution of wealth.[26] As political scientist Samuel H. Beer put it in his article, "Ronald

Reagan: New Deal Conservative?": "The New Deal was hammered out under the massive material blows of the Great Depression, inspiring a 'new brand of liberalism.' On the other hand, Lyndon Johnson's Great Society came in an era of affluence and featured federal technocrats carrying out 'social engineering.'"[27]

Reagan seemed willing to accept the economic security measures of the New Deal, including Social Security, but social engineering by federal bureaucrats was a different matter. For one thing, the country was not, in fact, in a permanent state of affluence as LBJ's economists had predicted. For another, these policies were not, as Charles Murray and others argued, effective in accomplishing their goals. Finally, Reagan saw them as undercutting individual freedom and opportunity. As Reagan's budget director David Stockman put it, a "safety net is different—it's the minimum to which you'll allow anyone to fall. To go beyond that and seek to level incomes is morally wrong and practically destructive."[28]

As a consequence, many of Reagan's tax and budget cuts were aimed at reducing or eliminating Great Society welfare programs, which had largely continued through the Nixon, Ford, and Carter years. The real (inflation-adjusted) rate of growth in federal spending dropped from 4 percent during the Carter years to 2.5 percent under Reagan. Notably, however, even Reagan could achieve only a drop in the rate of increase, not an actual reduction in federal spending. With stronger political support in Congress, he may have been able to do more. Certainly, tools he sought to wield but that he could not get past Congress—such as a balanced budget amendment or a line-item veto—might have made further difference.[29]

Reagan's tax policy started from the premise that lowering taxes left more money in people's pockets to pursue their own opportunities, rather than applying the money to government programs. The pursuit of happiness, a quest promised to people in the Declaration of Independence, should be a series of choices made by individuals, not government, he thought. Especially in a time of economic insecurity, this message resonated with voters. As Samuel H. Beer observed of Reagan's approach, "He seeks to shift social choice away from public choice and toward market choice."[30]

In addition to enhancing freedom and opportunity for individuals, Reagan argued, lowering taxes also boosted the troubled economy he had inherited from Jimmy Carter. In his acceptance speech at the 1980 Republican Convention, Reagan said, "We are taxing ourselves into economic exhaustion and stagnation, crushing our ability and incentive to save, invest and produce." Reagan argued that tax cuts even in the upper brackets were needed to unleash economic growth, in turn producing new jobs and greater savings.[31] Such economic opportunity derived from tax cuts would also help those who had less, Reagan argued. In the same convention speech, Reagan attacked the effect of tax increases on those who have less, saying his message would be, "We have to move ahead, but we're not going to leave anyone behind."

Lower taxes were part of what has come to be called the "supply-side economics" embraced in the Reagan era. Whereas Democrats followed the Keynesian philosophy of higher taxes and the redistribution of money to those less well off, Reagan's approach was to lower taxes and grow the economy instead.[32] The idea, credited to economist Arthur Laffer, was to count on economic growth to increase overall tax receipts, rather than keeping tax rates higher and subsequently slowing the economy. Such economic growth would lead to job growth as well, benefiting both those directly affected by the tax cuts and those whose job prospects would increase. This offered what appeared to be an attractive alternative to many in comparison with the older liberal idea of taxing the wealthy and redistributing money through federal programs and social engineering.[33]

Right along with reducing taxes, cutting government regulation was a key component of Reagan's economic and opportunity policies. Reagan felt that overregulation blocked entrepreneurial activity and was, therefore, a drag on job creation and economic growth. In his State of the Union address on February 4, 1986, for example, Reagan said, "Let us speak of our responsibility to redefine government's role: Not to control, not to demand or command but . . . to create a ladder of opportunity to full employment." He called this "providing new opportunity for all." In a message to the Conservative Political Action Committee (CPAC) on March 20, 1981, he touted the opportunity to replace "the overregulated society with the creative society." As political scientist John W. Sloan put it, "The Reagan Revolution vowed to lower oppressive tax burdens for all citizens and lift the deadweight of regulation from business."[34]

Reagan was fond of pointing out how Democrats, especially Lyndon Johnson, had created too many bureaucratic agencies and structures. Although greater regulation of the economy, the markets, and business had really begun with Franklin Roosevelt, Reagan thought Johnson had greatly accelerated it. Even before his presidency, in a speech to CPAC on January 25, 1974, Reagan said that during the Great Society, "There were eight cabinet departments and twelve independent agencies to administer the federal health programs. There were thirty-five housing programs and twenty transportation programs."

The Reagan counterrevolution tackled deregulation in a variety of ways. For example, his administration cut the budgets of regulatory agencies such as the Environmental Protection Agency, the Department of Energy, and the Occupational Health and Safety Administration by one-fourth.[35] He followed the 1980 Republican Party platform directive that "equal opportunity should not be jeopardized by bureaucratic regulations and decisions which rely on quotas, ratios, and numerical requirements," a phrase Reagan echoed during his campaign for the presidency, when he decried affirmative action's "bureaucratic regulations which rely on quotas, ratios and numerical requirements."[36] In Reagan's view, regulations both stunted the economic growth that created jobs and opportunity and also created discriminatory and destructive policies.

In many ways, Reagan's economic policies (often called Reaganomics) were at the heart of his efforts to restore equality of opportunity for Americans. When he summed up his administration's accomplishments in a radio address on January 2, 1988, he said, "We cut the number of government regulations and slowed the rate of growth of government itself. But most important, we reformed the tax code and cut individual income tax rates, restoring incentives for hard work, risk taking and innovation." A year later, in his farewell address of January 11, 1989, Reagan cited economic recovery through cutting taxes and regulation as one of the "great triumphs" of his presidency.

Franklin Roosevelt and Ronald Reagan were bookend presidents of the twentieth century. Each sought to transform public policy, and with it, the American system. Roosevelt's approach involved heavier taxation and federal spending in order to increase economic regulation and build a safety net for vulnerable Americans. Roosevelt's approach was based on the basic fairness of redistributing wealth from the "robber barons" to the "forgotten man."

Reagan, on the other hand, thought government's role should be more about growing the economic pie rather than regulating and redistributing the pie. In his 1974 CPAC speech, he said we "have distributed our wealth more widely among our people than any society known to man." Reagan's economic platform became, as his advisor Edwin Meese put it, "the centerpiece of the Reagan programs."[37] The troubled and unstable economy Reagan inherited from the 1970s, especially the part of the decade that covered Jimmy Carter's presidency, gave him the opportunity to refashion economic policy. As political scientist Mark A. Smith has argued, Reagan used the economic insecurity of the country, his powerful rhetorical skills, and new economic approaches to gain wide popularity for the conservative economic message.[38]

The speeches of Ronald Reagan, especially before his presidency and his use of White House speechwriters, were packed with stories and anecdotes he collected over the years and saved on note cards. One favorite captured his view of the role of economic freedom and growth. In his debate with George Bush in Houston in 1980, Reagan claimed, "If Americans since 1950 had been able to save and invest, if our economy had been able to grow at only one and a half percent more a year, our incomes would be 50 percent higher, jobs would be plentiful, we'd have a balanced budget."[39] This was a recurring Reagan theme: economic growth cured all ills.

The Republican platform of 1980, on which Reagan ran, highlighted this approach to the problems of Black Americans, for example, saying, "Our fundamental answer to the economic problems of black Americans is the same answer we make to all Americans—full employment without inflation through economic growth." The platform summarized the party's economic approach very clearly: "First and foremost, we are committed to a policy of economic expansion through tax-rate reductions, spending restraint, regulatory reform, and other incentives." In his first inaugural address, January 20, 1981, Reagan referred to a "growing economy that provides equal opportunity for all."

The Opportunity Society

Reagan felt the more powerful word in "equality of opportunity" was *opportunity*. One could argue that his Democratic predecessors Franklin Roosevelt and Lyndon Johnson were more interested in putting greater equality into opportunity, whereas Reagan felt that creating more opportunity raised all boats and, in that way, addressed the equality question even more effectively. It followed naturally from his economic program in that growing the economy, creating more jobs, and lowering taxes created more opportunity than redistributing a stagnant economy as Keynesians had been advocating and doing.

In Reagan's view, opportunity was what every American wanted, including minorities and those at a disadvantage economically. At the annual meeting of the NAACP in Denver, Colorado, on June 29, 1981, for example, Reagan contrasted Jimmy Carter's "'limits to growth' crowd" with his own view that "black Americans want what every other kind of American wants: a crack at a decent job, a home, safety in the streets and a good education for our children."[40] Repeatedly, he referred to these basic aspirations as opportunities. In his 1980 convention acceptance speech, he attacked the high tax rates of Democrats, saying it is like telling minorities who have reached the first rung of the "ladder of opportunity" that the ladder is being pulled out from under them. Likewise, the Republican platform of 1980 referred to the need to "pursue policies that will help make the opportunities of American life a reality for Hispanics." Reagan sought to characterize the Republican Party "as the instrument to bring about widespread economic growth and opportunity."[41]

In 1984, the year of his reelection campaign, Reagan introduced a new theme to describe his policies: "The opportunity society." A speech titled, "Our Noble Vision: An Opportunity Society for All," delivered at the CPAC annual dinner in 1984, laid out his vision. Reagan said that we are on a "mission" to promote the "revolutionary idea" of an "opportunity society" where "hope" reigns. He called the opportunity society a "noble vision" that begins with economic freedom and growth, and moves to freedom from crime and excellence in education. Like Reagan himself, the opportunity society is built on hope and optimism.

When he won reelection in 1984, his second inaugural address on January 21, 1985, called for "an American opportunity society in which all of us—white and black, rich and poor, young and old—will go forward together arm in arm." Reagan's February 6, 1985, State of the Union message continued with the opportunity society theme, calling for a "second Revolution of hope and opportunity," referring to "the magic of opportunity." He emphasized the need for "full economic power" for "blacks, Hispanics and all minorities." Clearly, his strategy was to replace government dependency with private opportunity.

Right along with tax cuts and economic growth, *opportunity* became one of the key terms in the Reagan vocabulary. What we want, he said in his January 25, 1984, State of the Union message, is "a society bursting with opportunities." After all, he said in an October 27, 1984, radio message, "The secret of America's success is opportunity." In both 1985 and 1986, he proposed a year of opportunity. Opportunities were to be available "for every American with nobody left behind," he said in a radio address on November 3, 1984. Near the end of his term, in a March 1987 speech to CPAC, "A Future That Works," he said Americans had "every reason to be optimistic" that we will prevail in our goal to secure a "strong, free and opportunity-filled" country.

Targeted Plans for Equality of Opportunity

In addition to his strategy of economic growth that would create opportunities for everyone, Reagan said and did more about creating greater equality than might generally be recognized. One could argue that Lyndon Johnson's expanded government programs to promote greater equality for certain groups had, even in Reagan's time, made continuing them in some form almost obligatory. That is to say that special government assistance for the poor and for

Blacks had become the new normal and, while Reagan did not emphasize that as much as LBJ, he nevertheless did not overlook it.

Reagan's equality plans began with a firm commitment to legal equality. He said in his first State of the Union address on January 26, 1982, "We must and shall see that those basic laws that guarantee equal rights are preserved and, when necessary, strengthened." Then, in a nod to women's rights that he would emphasize in his presidency, he added, "Our concern for equal rights for women is firm and unshakable." This, of course, solidified the first plank of Lyndon Johnson's own equality program, with laws that guaranteed equality in civil rights, voting rights, and the like.

Rhetorically, Reagan made it clear that he supported these disadvantaged groups in their efforts to achieve equality. In his 1980 Republican Convention acceptance speech, Reagan said, "We have to move ahead, but we're not going to leave anyone behind." He reiterated that theme in a November 3, 1984, radio address, saying we want "opportunities for every American with nobody left behind." He then elaborated that "nobody left behind means we must continue to modernize our older industries and rebuild our inner cities and distressed areas of America, so every American who wants a job can find a job." His diaries reflect frequent meetings with Black leaders from business and education. They also list a number of entries about women's rights and gender equality.

But Reagan could not support the second plank of Johnson's equality program: government planning and spending to create opportunities for certain groups of people, primarily Blacks and the poor. In a radio address on February 15, 1986, he made the point that Johnson's War on Poverty had failed, "in part because of helping the poor, government programs ruptured the bonds holding poor families together." He said that he was opposed to "bureaucratic regulations which rely on quotas, ratios and numerical requirements."[42]

President Reagan introduced a bill that suggests how his approach to helping low-income groups would be different from Johnson's: The Low-Income Opportunity Improvement Act of 1987. The bill was part of Reagan's larger welfare reform efforts, aimed at reducing both "poverty and dependency" as he said in a radio address on August 1, 1987. Reagan felt that the federal approach to poverty had become a "poverty trap" rather than an escape for the poor. He argued in his radio message that the key question was whether poverty policy helped people become "self-sufficient" or, alternatively, "[kept] them down in a state of dependency." Although the bill proposed several changes at the federal level, the heart of it was to encourage state and local governments to develop approaches that would reduce government dependency. The bill was merged into the Family Support Act of 1988 and enacted.

Reagan's different approach to welfare from that of Lyndon Johnson highlights again that Reagan saw Johnson's Great Society as posing far greater dangers to American values than Franklin Roosevelt's New Deal. Of course, Reagan began his political life as a Democrat and acknowledged that he had voted for Roosevelt four times. His father was aided by New Deal relief agencies and held a job in Roosevelt's Works Progress Administration.[43] Although Reagan later became, as his son Michael said, "disillusioned with FDR's Big Government policies,"[44] he nevertheless saw Roosevelt's policies as different in both kind and context from Lyndon Johnson's Great Society.

Reagan understood FDR's New Deal as primarily a series of economic security policies enacted during the frightening Great Depression. In that sense, they were really initiated out of economic necessity. In the case of Social Security, which was the primary "welfare" policy of the New Deal, it was paid for by worker contributions, so it could well be characterized as insurance, not as true welfare. Johnson's War on Poverty and Great Society, however, were different for Reagan. These policies were enacted not in a time of national need, but during an era of economic plenty. Their purpose was not to provide security or insurance, but rather equality. As Reagan's budget director, David Stockman, put it, "I don't accept that equality is a moral principle. . . . That's the overlay, the idea around the welfare state. A safety net is different."[45]

Reagan accepted the Roosevelt safety net, but not Johnson's redistribution of wealth and controlling planners. He said in his 1980 convention acceptance speech that the country needed "both the forward momentum of economic growth and the strength of the safety net beneath those in society who need help." He added that "it is essential that the integrity of all aspects of Social Security are preserved." Reagan even took the initiative to strengthen the safety net to cover the elderly who suffered catastrophic illnesses, as he revealed in a February 14, 1987, radio address. This was enacted through the Medicare Catastrophic Coverage Act of 1988 (although it was largely repealed the following year).

The Great Society, however, was cut from an entirely different cloth, in Reagan's view. It was about government spending and planning to "improve" the lives of people, which, as Reagan saw it, took away too much individual freedom while creating too much government control. Because Johnson saw poverty as both an economic and a social challenge, his solutions necessarily brought the federal government more deeply into those issues. As Samuel H. Beer summarized it, "Because of this definition of the problem and its consequent stress on technocratic actors and solutions, the Great Society, in contrast to the New Deal, led to a far greater emphasis on public expenditure as the basic mode of government action."[46] As a consequence, Reagan's budget cuts were aimed more at Great Society programs and barely touched Social Security and New Deal initiatives.[47]

Conclusion

In the end, Ronald Reagan's counterrevolution said and did more about opportunity than about equality per se. Reagan's theory was that if you raised all ships through a robust economy fueled by tax cuts and job growth, it would help those who were unequal as well as those better off. He felt that creating more and better jobs would especially target and help those at the bottom of the economic ladder. At the same time, he was highly critical of federal efforts to micromanage the lives of the poor through various government programs, and was quick to point out their failures.

In a larger sense, Reagan also felt his approach to opportunity was much more consistent with American values than Lyndon Johnson's policies toward the poor and the unequal. Herbert Hoover, who coined the term "rugged individualism," and paired it with "equality of opportunity" to describe the American system, spent his post-presidential years decrying the loss of individualism and the rise of collectivism inherent in New Deal policies. George H. Nash quotes Hoover as telling an associate in the early days of the New Deal: "'The impending battle in this country' would be between 'a properly regulated individualism' and 'sheer socialism.' That was 'likely to be the great political battle for some years to come.'"[48] This indeed could well describe the ongoing debates between the right and left even today.

Samuel H. Beer described this same dilemma as "the balance sought between individualism and intervention," noting that "when he took office, Ronald Reagan" sought to "shift the balance toward individualism." Or, as Beer described it in economic terms, Reagan sought to "shift social choice away from public choice and toward market choice."[49] While experts debate which approach—economic growth and greater opportunity, or greater government intervention in favor of the poor—made more of a difference in creating equality of opportunity, there is also this larger philosophical question of what kind of political values the US chooses to embrace. Reagan's choice in favor of freedom, individualism, and economic growth was clear, and clearly at odds with Lyndon Johnson's Great Society. But then who would have thought that Founding arguments of self-reliance and individual effort would prevail shortly in the 1996 Welfare Reform Act, moving families "from welfare to work"? And more than that, who was prepared for the soon-to-be President Bill Clinton to declare that the era of big government was over?

Notes

1. Julian Zelizer, *The Fierce Urgency of Now* (New York: Penguin Books, 2015), 317.
2. Zelizer, 319.
3. Dean J. Kotlowski, "Richard Nixon and the Origins of Affirmative Action," *The Historian* 60, no. 3 (Spring 1998): 523–41. See also Kevin Yuill, *Richard Nixon and the Rise of Affirmative Action: The Pursuit of Equality in an Era of Limits* (Lanham, MD: Rowman & Littlefield, 2006).
4. "Where the Quotas Came From," *Fortune* (May 30, 1994): 199.
5. George H. Nash, *The Conservative Intellectual Movement in America* (Wilmington, DE: Basic Books, 2008), 259.

6. Pat Buchanan, *Nixon's White House Wars* (New York: Crown Forum, 2017), 26, 45.

7. Martin Anderson, *Revolution: The Reagan Legacy* (Stanford, CA: Hoover Institution Press, 1988), 17–18.

8. Mark A. Smith, *The Right Talk: How Conservatives Transformed the Great Society Into the Economic Society* (Princeton, NJ: Princeton University Press, 2007), 72.

9. Nash, *Conservative Intellectual Movement*, 336.

10. Charles Murray, *Losing Ground: American Social Policy, 1950–1980* (New York: Basic Books, 1984).

11. Murray, 8.

12. Michael Harrington, *The Other America: Poverty in the United States* (New York: The MacMillan Company, 1962).

13. Murray, *Losing Ground,* 69.

14. Murray, 69.

15. John W. Sloan, *FDR and Reagan: Transformative Presidents with Clashing Visions* (Lawrence, KS: University Press of Kansas, 2008), 341.

16. Gordon Lloyd and David Davenport, *The New Deal and Modern American Conservatism: A Defining Rivalry* (Stanford, CA: Hoover Institution Press, 2013).

17. Gordon Lloyd and David Davenport, "The Two Phases of Herbert Hoover's Constitutional Conservatism," in *Toward an American Conservatism: Constitutional Conservatism During the Progressive Era*, ed. Joseph Postell and Johnathan O'Neill (New York: Palgrave MacMillan, 2013).

18. George H. Nash, *The Crusade Years, 1933–1955: Herbert Hoover's Lost Memoir of the New Deal and Its Aftermath* (Stanford, CA: Hoover Institution Press, 2013).

19. Gordon Lloyd, ed., *The Two Faces of Liberalism: How the Hoover-Roosevelt Debate Shapes the 21st Century* (Salem, MA: M&M Scrivener Press, 2007).

20. George H. Nash, *Reappraising the Right: The Past and Future of American Conservatism* (Wilmington, DE: ISI Books, 2009), 319.

21. Nash, *Conservative Intellectual Movement*, 180–81.

22. Thomas W. Evans, *The Education of Ronald Reagan: The General Electric Years and the Untold Story of His Conversion to Conservatism* (New York: Columbia University Press, 2006).

23. Douglas Brinkley, ed., *The Reagan Diaries* (New York: HarperCollins Publishers, 2007), 96.

24. Jonathan Darman, *Landslide: LBJ and Ronald Reagan at the Dawn of a New America* (New York: Random House, 2014), xxviii.

25. Brinkley, *Reagan Diaries*, 65.

26. See, e.g., Sloan, *FDR and Reagan*, 3, 360.

27. Samuel H. Beer, "Ronald Reagan: New Deal Conservative?," *Society* 20, no. 2 (January 1983): 40–44.

28. Sloan, *FDR and Reagan*, 316.

29. A line-item veto bill was enacted later, in 1996, but was declared unconstitutional by the Supreme Court.

30. Beer, "Ronald Reagan," 41.

31. Smith, *Right Talk*, 111, 113.

32. Anderson, *Revolution*, 284.

33. Marc G. Worthy, "An Examination of Tax Law and Supply Side Economics: Creed of Greed or Opportunity for All," *North Dakota Law Review* 72, no. 3 (1996): 691, 694–95.

34. Sloan, *FDR and Reagan*, 10.

35. Livia Gershon, "Why Ronald Reagan Became the Great Deregulator," *JSTOR Daily*, February 9, 2017.

36. Frank Dobbin, *Inventing Equal Opportunity* (Princeton, NJ: Princeton Press, 2009), 136.

37. Sloan, *FDR and Reagan*, 223.

38. Smith, *Right Talk*, 14, 72, 104–05.

39. Rick Perlstein, *Reaganland: America's Right Turn 1976–1980* (New York: Simon & Schuster, 2020), 776.

40. Quoted in Craig Shirley, *Reagan Risking: The Decisive Years 1976–1980* (New York: Broadside Books, 2017), 104.

41. Quoted in Sloan, *FDR and Reagan*, 37.

42. Dobbin, *Inventing Equal Opportunity*, 136.

43. Sloan, *FDR and Reagan,* 84.

44. Michael Reagan, *The New Reagan Revolution* (New York: Thomas Dunne Books, 2010), 113.

45. Sloan, *FDR and Reagan*, 316.

46. Beer, "Ronald Reagan," 43.

47. Beer, 43.

48. Nash, *Reappraising the Right*, 257.

49. Beer, "Ronald Reagan," 41.

CHAPTER FIVE

Whatever Happened to Equality of Opportunity?

Americans have consistently said they believe in the principle of equality of opportunity. As the authors of a Brookings Institution study on the subject concluded: "Americans believe in opportunity. . . . They are far more interested in equal opportunity than in equal results."[1] The Pew Research Center and, more recently, the State Policy Network confirm that it remains a strong American value.[2] These days, however, that notion is under constant challenge and even attack. There are philosophical debates proposing major revisions to traditional understandings of equality of opportunity. Indeed, there are suggestions that these be scrapped and replaced with newer ideas such as equity or equality of outcome. Equality of opportunity is also challenged on the policy front, with proposed new economic and social plans that would move America down a very different path. In this chapter, we will try to understand where equality of opportunity stands today, what philosophical and policy challenges it now faces, and what direction it could and should take for the future.

As we have noted, there has been a long-standing debate between the Founders' understanding of equality of opportunity and that of Progressives. Essentially, the Founders believed equality was a natural right, an endowment from the creator. "All men are created equal," they stated in the Declaration of

Independence. Equality was something you moved from in building out your life, and it was the role of government to guard and protect that right. The Progressives accepted, perhaps grudgingly, that that might have been sufficient in an earlier day but, with the closing of the American frontier and the arrival of industrialization, equality of opportunity was no longer freely available. It had become, according to the Progressives, something America could no longer assume but rather had to create, with the role of the federal government in developing greater equality becoming central.

While this fundamental debate continues today, there are important new philosophical terms used to define and understand equality of opportunity, especially equality of outcomes and equity. The proper role of government in pursuing equality of opportunity is also an increasingly important and contentious question. In our search for whatever became of equality of opportunity, we turn to these philosophical debates of the day, beginning with a fundamental question: Equality of what?

Equality of Opportunity Versus Equality of Outcome

One longtime debate is whether America seeks to pursue equality of opportunity or equality of outcome or results. As noted in chapter 3, some argue that Lyndon Johnson actually moved the equality bar from opportunity to outcomes in his Great Society poverty programs—but we are not so sure. A more defensible conclusion would be that Johnson chose to look at outcomes in deciding whether equality of opportunity was being achieved, rather than targeting equal outcomes as a policy result. That is an especially important and useful distinction today.

The argument today seems to be that, if equality of opportunity was once the goal, it is no longer enough and we should move on to the more robust equality of outcomes as a policy goal. In the 2020 presidential campaign, vice presidential candidate Kamala Harris called for this kind of change, saying in a campaign video about equality that "we [should] all end up at the same place."[3] She argued that if two people had the same opportunity, but began from a different starting point, the results would not be equal as they should be. All this is often described in the context of a race.[4] If everyone begins from the same starting point, there is equality of opportunity, but what if they do not? The primary equalizer of the starting point has been education, so that has been accepted as consistent with equality of opportunity. But then what if those in the race exert different levels of effort? Does the government then need to step in and equalize the outcome? In the common understanding of equality of opportunity, that would not be an appropriate adjustment.

Equality of outcomes has experienced a renewal of interest during the social justice movements of the 2020s. For example, Kent State professor of African American history Elizabeth M. Smith-Pryor has written that equality of opportunity may have worked for Whites but is a myth for Blacks, calling for "equality of results" as "a more concrete response to our current yet long-standing crisis."[5] As she pointed out, equality of results will require major structural changes in both our economic and social policies. If shifting from equality of opportunity to equality of results is a dramatic change—and it is—modern proponents say American society is in need of that type of bold transformation. As we shall see in the policy proposals below, this sort of equality debate argues that education as an adjustment to equality of opportunity to promote greater fairness is not enough; there must be economic equalizers as well.

The other side of this debate argues that equality of opportunity is not only the American tradition, but it remains a valid goal. The core argument is that making people's lives and circumstances turn out equally is virtually impossible and that government, in particular, would not be able to accomplish this. There are difficult definitional questions: How do we define equality of outcomes? Is it purely a financial matter, or are there social, educational, and other elements involved? Then, how do we account for individual choices that people make? One may choose to be a teacher or a butcher, for example, accepting for his or her own reasons that these professions will pay less than being a doctor or a rock star. How do we factor in talent or ability? Most of us do not possess the talent of LeBron James or Tom Brady, for example, and will be unable to earn the millions paid to many professional athletes. And what will happen to liberty if we, in effect, disconnect it from equality and allow the government to decide what equality means and how it will be achieved?

There is also a lively argument about the extent to which different outcomes are necessarily unfair or created by unfairness. Economists have pointed out, for example, that much of the gap in earnings between White and Black workers is explained by variables such as education, test scores, and work experience.[6] If, as labor economist Harry Holzer suggested, "Differences in educational attainment and test scores together may account for most of the racial differences in earnings,"[7] that would suggest a different policy approach than trying to equalize bottom-line incomes.

Then there are questions of fairness in a system of equality of outcomes. Equality of outcomes requires that individuals and groups of people be treated unequally, giving more to some and less to others, taking from some to give to others. Does government really belong in the business of taking money from someone who devoted his or her life to developing a particular talent or career and giving it to someone who did not make such a commitment? As Milton and Rose Friedman concluded, "The ethical issues [in equality of outcome] involved are subtle and complex."[8]

Is pursuing equality of outcomes consistent with the American understanding of liberty as well as equality? Is America ready to trade in being "the land of opportunity," still sought after by millions of immigrants, in order to pursue only equality? Should government be in the business of equalizing people's economic or social status, and could it even accomplish that if it sought to do so? Could America withstand such a shock to its system? These questions suggest that the country is not likely to move aggressively toward equality of outcomes, at least not any time soon.

Equality of Opportunity Versus Equity

A more current debate, but one that actually follows similar lines of argument that support equality of outcomes, concerns equity. Equity seems to be the new code word to describe the pursuit of a more just society and the new replacement for equality of opportunity as a goal. We need "equity" for people of color, for women, for transgender individuals, and others—these are the claims of the day. Some say we need it because equality of opportunity is no longer sufficient. Others say we need both equality and equity.

The increasing and current use of the term *equity* is puzzling, because it is not clear what it means or how it may be different, if it is, from equality. The term has a history of use in finances to denote the building of capital. The first definition in the Merriam-Webster dictionary is simply "justice according to natural law or right." Scholar Shelby Steele, reviewing its previous meaning, says the current use of the term "has no meaning."[9] Perhaps it derives from a sense that a new term is needed for marketing purposes, or because the term *equality* hasn't really accomplished all it should.[10]

In any event, as used today, equity sounds like a call for something stronger and bolder than equality of opportunity. It seems to focus more on equal results than merely equal opportunity. Equity appears to seek something grander in scale, something more connected to justice than mere fairness or opportunity. President Biden, and other government leaders, have begun to use the term in stating broader social justice goals. In any event, it seems like it will need to develop a much clearer meaning, at least in policy terms if not in a legal understanding, before it can truly be a game changer. Presently it clouds and obscures equality of opportunity but it has not replaced it.

The Proper Role of Government

At the same time as we ask these newer philosophical questions—mostly concerning whether equality of opportunity is still a sufficient goal in our society—we continue to face the question debated by the Founders and Progressives about the proper role of government in equality. Conservatives argue that America is fundamentally built on individual liberty and that the proper role of government is to protect that. Liberals, on the other hand, argue that individual freedom has led to too much inequality, especially inequality of income and wealth, and that only the government has the power to step in and correct these inequalities. In some ways, the history of the last century has been one of increasing the government's role in favor of greater equality, with occasional returns to the primacy of individual liberty promoted by the Founders.

How this debate is resolved depends primarily on one's political preference: conservatism or liberalism. As a starting point, we have noted that the American people stand behind the notion of equality of opportunity as a goal or aspiration that reflects the Declaration of Independence, the Constitution, and the American dream. But then the question arises—is there anything government should do to increase equality? Should it spend more on education, for example, especially in communities where a good education is not readily accessible? That bridge seems to have been crossed and the consensus is yes, greater support for education in poor communities is appropriate. Should there be civil rights laws, supported by court decisions, that expand equality in voting, jobs, and ethnic and gender rights? Again, the general consensus has been yes, this kind of government intervention to promote legal and social equality is appropriate, even when we do not always agree on the specific policies.

Next has come a series of initiatives to use the government to bring about greater equality for groups of people: senior citizens, those living in poverty, the disabled, those who cannot afford health care, and so on. On these questions, there has been some consensus, but not entirely so. It really began with Franklin Roosevelt's New Deal and the development of Social Security to afford special protections to the elderly, though this was a milder form of government support since it operated as a kind of insurance, collecting money from people in their working years and returning it with increased value in their later years. It really fell to Lyndon Johnson's Great Society of the 1960s to accelerate government intervention in providing equalizing assistance to groups of people seen as needing that boost. The Great Society premise was LBJ's view that, as he stated in his 1965 Howard University commencement address, it wasn't enough to open the door of opportunity, but you had to have a real chance to walk through it. This would require extra government assistance if you had been held down by poverty or racism, and his Great Society implemented many such programs, especially its War on Poverty and related job and education efforts. Johnson also expanded support for seniors with the implementation of Medicare. Critics questioned whether government should be discriminating in favor of certain groups, as well as whether government could actually accomplish any meaningful leveling of the playing field in this way. The results of Johnson's programs were mixed at best.

Perhaps the only president who tacked back in the direction of the Founders' understanding of equality of opportunity was Ronald Reagan. His view was that government not only should not but could not effectively create equality of opportunity. He famously said that the government had declared war on poverty but that poverty had won. He called out the expanding welfare state as opposed to the "spirit of 1776." Government was not, he famously said, the solution to the problem, "government is the problem." Reagan's understanding of what he called "the opportunity society" was to shrink government and its taxation so that it got out of the way of people's individual freedom and choices, including the freedom to pursue their own opportunities. In particular, Reagan objected to government planners who ran programs trying to direct the choices and opportunities that individuals might make. He felt real opportunity was the ability to make one's own choices.

By and large, however, the policy debate since the time of Franklin Roosevelt has not been whether but how much government can and should help those needing special assistance. The welfare state has continued to grow, with President George W. Bush adding prescription drug benefits for seniors and President Barack Obama's sweeping health care reform, delivering government-funded health care to millions in need. Obamacare was widely criticized as a move toward socialized medicine and away from individual liberty, but it did stop short of creating single-payer (that is, completely provided or funded by the government) health care. So long as these expansive government programs allowed room for the private sector, it was arguably still consistent with the liberty narrative. Thus did Lyndon Johnson's Medicare and Barack Obama's health care leave room for private insurance and doctors, for example.

It seems likely that this could be the continuing debate for a long time: How far can the government go in providing aid and leveling the playing field without violating the individual liberties of the Founding? Or, at what point have we really left equality of opportunity and allowed government to manage some sort of equality of outcome or results? This paradigm allows room for both the Founding view and the Progressive view to be constantly debated and managed as new government programs arise.

In the twenty-first century, however, the terms of the debate have shifted quite dramatically. With proposals that government must tackle income inequality, or even wealth inequality, the pendulum is shifting away from equality of opportunity to something else. In the argument that we should not only try to bring disadvantaged people's income and wealth up, but that government should, in fairness, also be bringing top earners' incomes down, opportunity is clearly under challenge. It is in this arena of economic equality that the doctrine of equality of opportunity could finally be struck a kind of death blow, and to these policy proposals we now turn.

Thomas Piketty and Economic Equality

If, as we argued in chapter 1, Woodrow Wilson turned Progressives of the early twentieth century toward a new and different kind of equality of opportunity, the French economist Thomas Piketty is the harbinger of an even more progressive equality now in the early twenty-first century. The new progressive equality concerns itself primarily with income and wealth, arguing that until those are addressed, there is no real equality in our society. Piketty's three books—the latest one on equality specifically—stake out this bold progressive ground.[11] No longer will political or legal equality, or education delivering equality of opportunity, be sufficient until bold plans are undertaken to address inequality of income and wealth. This, of course, would change the entire equality of opportunity debate.

Piketty's view of history, not unlike our own, sees a long march toward equality through the twentieth century until the Reagan counterrevolution of the 1980s. Piketty presents extensive data showing a dramatic rise in global wealth since the 1980s, due especially to inherited wealth and investment gains, unrelated to work or effort, which he calls "patrimonial capitalism."[12] Reagan's tax reforms and a general return to liberty over the former "great passion for equality" set both income and wealth inequality on their own long march.[13] Piketty argued that government's normal fiscal and social tools would not be enough to address this new, sweeping inequality.[14] Instead, he proposed, there needed to be "a progressive global tax on capital," not so much to "finance the social state but to regulate capitalism."[15] In other words, the point was not to seek greater wealth equality by giving to those with less, but it was even more important to take money from those who had more—obviously a revolutionary shift in one's understanding of equality and the government's role in it. Piketty seeks "confiscatory rates" on top incomes.[16]

In a real sense, Piketty's starting point for this economic revolution is not the American Revolution of 1776 but the French Revolution of 1789. He draws upon the first two sentences of the French Declaration of Rights of 1789: "Men are born and remain free and equal in rights. Social distinctions may be based only on common utility." It is this notion of common utility, or what is best for the society as a whole, that drives Piketty's economic and social conclusions. There is, for him, no other justification for how wealth and income should be distributed. As a consequence, he would replace existing Western economies with a form of "participatory socialism and social federalism."[17]

Piketty's most recent book, *A Brief History of Equality* (2022), argues that the whole idea of human progress is to move toward greater equality.[18] But he does not refer to equality of opportunity, but rather equality as a matter of power. Piketty seeks to track "the evolution of access to concrete goods such as education, health care, food, clothing, housing, transportation, culture, and so on,"[19] all with an eye toward "justice" (not opportunity) as the goal.[20] His concern is that the move toward equality was halted in the 1980s by Ronald Reagan, Margaret Thatcher, and other conservative political leaders.[21] Since then, the wealthy have become inordinately wealthier and are not paying their fair share. This is also seen in what he calls the "patrimonial middle class" with its real estate holdings and inherited wealth.[22] These problems will require strengthening the welfare state to be sure, but more than that, a system of highly progressive taxation to transform capitalism.[23]

Piketty seeks something well beyond equality of opportunity. He is pursuing nothing less than a complete reordering of the economic system. He is as much or more concerned with taking power and money from the wealthy than he is creating greater opportunity for the poor. The levers he would push are power, justice, capitalism, and wealth, not mere opportunity. In that sense Piketty has staked out a ground well beyond the Progressives of previous eras. And one does see signs that some progressive politicians are paying attention. Senator Bernie Sanders, for example, has advocated a special tax "on the extreme wealth of the top 0.1%."[24] Sanders's concern is not how much this would help the poor; rather, his stated objective is "to reduce the outrageous level of inequality" and "to rebuild the disappearing middle class."[25] Like Piketty, his goals are about power and inequality. President Joe Biden has jumped on this bandwagon, proposing his own new tax on billionaires (based not just on income, but also wealth).[26] These moves are short of Piketty's call for an economic revolution, but they advance his core thinking about power, wealth, capitalism, and inequality.

Guaranteed Minimum Income

A less radical economic approach is providing people a guaranteed minimum income, or universal basic income. Under this kind of plan, everyone receives a monthly stipend, often around $500, to provide enough of a base to build on, or a stream of income to fill gaps or deal with emergencies. Even the conservative economist Milton Friedman advocated a form of this—the negative income tax—decades ago, and Andrew Yang promoted it as one of his core ideas in the presidential campaign of 2020. The basic questions are who should be eligible—is it truly universal or should it be targeted at lower-income recipients—and who would pay for this?

In our system of federalism, this idea is being tested in pilot programs around the country. One report suggested that there are more than eighty guaranteed-income pilots[27] and another article listed thirty-three current or recent programs in the US.[28] In addition to a number of smaller pilot programs, large cities such as Chicago and Los Angeles are experimenting with this, especially during the COVID-19 emergency. The city of Stockton, California, has studied the effects of its program, reporting significant positive outcomes for families and individuals, without some of the expected downsides.[29] This is an approach to addressing poverty and increasing equality of opportunity that deserves further study and careful testing.

Equality of Opportunity: Can It Be Saved? Should It?

On one end of the spectrum we can see traditional equality of opportunity as envisioned and embraced by the Founders. In this view, men and women are created equal, and therefore have equal rights, especially political and legal rights. From that starting point, people are free to make their own choices on how to, as the Declaration of Independence put it, pursue happiness. Guaranteeing individual rights, so that people are free to choose, is the primary role of government in this traditional view of equality of opportunity. Paring back the role of government regulation in people's lives, reducing taxes, and promoting individual freedom was President Ronald Reagan's path back toward this more traditional view, and many conservatives still advocate this today.

On the other side—not quite the other end of the spectrum—is the liberal view that there is so much inequality in the world that government must play an active role in addressing it. Education is a primary way of creating greater and more equal opportunity and this, of course, is a government responsibility. Even conservatives or traditionalists agree with that. There are arguments about how to go about using education to create more equal opportunity, such as the role of affirmative action, for example. But there is broad concurrence that education is a highly leveraged tool for creating greater and more equal opportunity.

But liberals go beyond education and argue that the government must engage in programs to increase equality of opportunity for the poor and disadvantaged, and also for ethnic groups that have been left behind in society. Lyndon Johnson's Great Society sought to move the federal government strongly in this direction, but history suggests that it is very difficult for government to move the opportunity and equality needles. Government programs fight poverty, racism, and a variety of social and economic ills, yet these problems persist. Still, this is where the equality of opportunity debate has been playing out for the last fifty to sixty years. Government keeps adding to the social safety net and building out the welfare state in the hope of creating greater equality of opportunity. Do we need to add universal health care to the social and economic agenda? Should we pay off everyone's college debt? Conservatives argue that this is not the proper role of government and such programs do not work, but the debate and policy implementation continue.

Now, several movements on the left have created a new end of the Progressive spectrum—perhaps we could call it a super-progressive stance on equality, or the new New Left. The income inequality movement has brought to the fore difficult questions about equality, and has called into question whether those in a shrinking middle class and a growing lower class will have sufficient opportunities without a radical change to capitalism and taxation. Then, too, Black Lives Matter and social justice movements have questioned whether equality of opportunity is a sufficient goal; whether we need to be pursuing something else such as equality of outcomes or vague notions of equity. So all of that has created a new Progressive view at the far end of the spectrum from the Founding position.

The political question then becomes whether this is an either/or choice. Is it either the Founding/conservative view or the Progressive/liberal view? Or is there room for some kind of middle ground that would become the future for equality of opportunity? To this important question we now turn.

A Modern Middle Ground?

In an era in which political compromise has become a dirty word, and finding common ground a fruitless search, we ask whether equality of opportunity might be a base from which both liberals and conservatives could work. To be sure, with liberty comes inequality but, by now, almost any inequality is seen as the enemy of democracy. Can we find trade-offs that would permit both conservatives and liberals to embrace equality of opportunity and, if we found such middle ground conceptually, could the two sides agree to occupy and work from it?

We might begin by understanding that the sustaining value of the Founding view is, as the name of its proponents suggests, as a foundation or a point of departure, a framework from which to work. America is still, aspirationally at least, a land of liberty and equality. While there is often a tension between the two, we have lived with and found energy in that dilemma since the Founding. The cornerstone of this, from the Declaration of Independence, is that everyone is "created equal" and at liberty to pursue their own opportunities to secure "Life, Liberty and Happiness." Since a dilemma involves two or more values in tension that nevertheless need to work together, dropping one value in favor of the other will be a mistake. Neither pursuing liberty without attention to equality nor equality without due commitment to liberty is the American way. Equality of opportunity, then, is how America, since the Founding, has managed that dilemma, by supporting the liberty to find opportunity, but doing so in a way that supports greater equality. Equality of opportunity is not something a society finally achieves, but it is both a tool with which it works and an aspiration to pursue. It is this understanding that, at least conceptually, creates the platform on which both conservatives and liberals may continue to embrace and work on the concept of equality of opportunity.

Progressives argue that equality of opportunity was no longer available to individuals without substantial government support once the American frontier had closed. But frontiers need not be only geographical—indeed, there are many new frontiers today creating new opportunities. Immigrants see opportunity here and move here in search of it. Technology has created entire new fields of opportunity to which young people, especially, have flocked. Certain states and sections of the country are seen as new frontiers of opportunity and people are relocating there. So, yes, even from the point of view of frontiers, opportunity is still alive and well.

The liberal view today, focusing on income inequality and social justice, might be best understood as a set of important questions about equality of opportunity, rather than a replacement. Piketty and others ask how can we say there is equality of opportunity when the wealthy have more and more opportunity and the middle and lower classes, at least in relative terms, have less. Although we are not likely to follow the lead of a French economist more committed to the French Revolution than the American one, he and his colleagues nevertheless pose important questions. The same is true for the several movements that ask how we can say there is equal justice when certain ethnic and socioeconomic groups are not treated equally by the police and other government and social entities. Again, this is a difficult and important set of questions for a maturing democracy to address. Before we throw over nearly 250-year-old economic and political systems, we should begin by seeing what answers American democratic capitalism might have for these questions.

This brings us to a middle ground, where the future of equality of opportunity is likely to be worked out. If people just hold to their extreme positions, a middle ground will not be found. But if they can break through their own particular understandings and rhetoric, then a consensus, a middle ground, is possible. It is this deliberate sense of the community—not the extremes—that will lead us to greater equality of opportunity.

Is Opportunity Still Important?

First, let us ask whether America continues to be a land of opportunity, which is a central question to be sorted out on this middle ground. These days far more attention is paid to the equality dimension than the opportunity element of our theme, so is opportunity still relevant and important? Interestingly, the strongest possible answer comes from immigrants who overwhelmingly state that this is why they have come to America—for opportunity. Two economists, from Stanford and Princeton, have recently pulled together what they call "the first truly big set of data about immigration" from census records, presenting them in their new book: *Streets of Gold: America's Untold Story of Immigrant Success.*[30] They found that second-generation immigrants, especially, found strong job and economic opportunities in the US and, in fact, outperformed native-born Americans. The children of immigrants did not face as many language or educational limitations as their parents and, unlike many native-born Americans, their families tended to settle where jobs were available. As co-author Ran Abramitzky said, "The American dream is just as alive now as it was a century ago."[31]

One aspect of the opportunity difference between immigrants and the native-born is the comparison group. To the extent immigrants are comparing their opportunities to those in their native countries, America seems very much like a land of opportunity. Greater entrepreneurship, lower tax rates, reduced regulation, and fewer barriers to good jobs all contribute to the greater opportunity immigrants experience coming to the US. A recent study by the Pew Research Center shows additional advantages in the US that cause Latin Americans to immigrate.[32] To the extent that native-born Americans compare their opportunities to those of wealthier people in the news, of course, their opportunities seem fewer. Compared to what, or to whom, then, is an important question.

As noted in the *Streets of Gold* study, however, another important factor is immigrants' willingness to move geographically toward opportunity. Native-born children feel attachments to community and family that make them less mobile than immigrants who have already left home and are on the move. As economist Raj Chetty concluded in a 2021 study, however, neighborhood and community are huge factors in delivering opportunity for the next generation. Chetty observed that growing up in neighborhoods where people were working is key to developing opportunities for kids.[33] Chetty goes so far as to propose that moving kids to successful working neighborhoods is a more powerful tool than trying to change existing neighborhoods, since we do not understand all the problems and how to change them.[34] Indeed, this is precisely what immigrant families do.

The huge demand from immigrants to come to America and find greater opportunity is one piece of evidence that opportunity still works and remains a key to the American dream. Another is economic mobility. While certain studies have shown growth in economic inequality, other studies have shown that economic mobility—the ability to move from one quadrant of income to another—is still alive in America. While it has been widely reported that today's youth are less likely to make more money than their parents, recent studies show that this is not the case.[35] Further, while it is true that incomes at the top have grown faster than those at the bottom, there has nevertheless been income growth throughout.[36] While income equality is an unrealistic and undemocratic goal, income mobility is desirable in creating opportunity and further developments in the field should emphasize this. One interesting proposal is to create an index showing how much particular colleges and universities increase the income mobility of their graduates; the colleges that rank high in this area are not necessarily the most famous schools.[37] Increased attention needs to be given to how to create greater income and economic mobility.

Perhaps the most important factor in developing opportunity, and one that finds broad support in the middle ground, is education. This is where both liberals and conservatives agree and could work even more effectively together. Focusing on opportunity for children is the greatest long-term investment a society can make in its future. Indeed, it is the essence of the American dream. As President Barack Obama said in his second inaugural address: "We are true to our creed when a little girl born into the bleakest poverty knows that she has the same chance to succeed as anybody else, because she is an American; she is free, and she is equal, not just in the eyes of God but also in our own."

Economist Joseph Stiglitz, a critic of income inequality from the left, has acknowledged that, "Probably the most important reason for lack of equality of opportunity is education: both its quantity and quality."[38] Likewise, conservatives who believe in relying on greater individualism understand that preparing and empowering students is a better solution to our problems than higher taxation, regulation, or other government initiatives. Left and right will differ on precisely how to improve education, but the notion that education is central to creating greater opportunity is widely shared. Unfortunately, however, America has been shifting its spending priorities away from the young and toward the old. As former Stanford University president John Hennessy has said, "The shift in where our national investment goes is a tragedy. . . . We have dramatically shifted who we are trying to help in this country, I think to the detriment of young people. The inability of government to deal with entitlements is increasing a burden on others, including investing in young people, who are the future."[39]

If we are looking where to invest in education to create greater opportunity, the leverage points would appear to be preschool, high school, and college. Studies show that early intervention in a child's learning is key to the entire educational cycle.[40] Then, too, there is increasing attention to the need to create multiple pathways toward opportunity in work during high school, not just a single route to college.[41] Finally, as 80 percent of Americans continue to believe, college has become an increasingly vital experience for young people who are seeking greater opportunity in life and more pathways need to be opened there, especially at the community college level.[42] Both from the left and right there can be agreement that education is where great minds and substantial investment need to be applied in order to create what Ronald Reagan called "an opportunity society."

Then, too, we need to consider how education can help build up equality of opportunity within the American system rather than tearing it down. A variety of attacks on the Founding and the American system have found their way into the educational curriculum, beginning with Howard Zinn's *A People's History of the United States*, now a popular textbook highly critical of nearly everything about America and its history. The 1619 Project seeks to reset the founding of America to coincide with slavery and change the American narrative. Critical race theory, action civics, and other critiques of America abound in K–12 education. It is hard to love an ugly Founding and, to the extent that education portrays America as ugly, biased, and prejudiced, we will not be raising up generations of citizens who love and want to contribute to America.

Moving Toward Greater Equality

As we noted in chapter 1, equality has long been debated by the Founders and Progressives. To the Founders, equality was a self-evident truth, something one moved from into the world to make life choices in the pursuit of happiness. A century or more later, the Progressives said no, we can no longer assume equality (if we ever could); rather, it has become something we must take steps toward, and government should lead the way in providing it. The role of government, Progressives argued, could no longer be limited to guaranteeing political freedom, but rather it must reach out to establish legal, social, and economic freedom as well.

By now, it seems fair to acknowledge that Progressives have won that argument. For the last one hundred years and still counting, the question is no longer *whether* government should take a leading role in seeking to guarantee equality, but rather *how far* in that direction it should go and how much it can and should do. One could argue that a series of presidents, beginning with Franklin Roosevelt, have sought to increase the government's role in creating greater economic security, as well as legal and social equality. Conservatives are left to argue: Don't go too far! Don't completely eliminate American individualism and the liberty for people to pursue happiness each in their own way. Noted conservative William F. Buckley observed this role for conservatives, saying that basically they "stand athwart history yelling Stop." Ronald Reagan is the only president since the 1930s who has successfully both argued and taken action toward returning government to the more limited role envisioned by the Founders.

The policy debate about equality between the Progressives and Founders has therefore become a limited one of how and how far, not whether government should be active in delivering equality. The questions on the table have been along these lines: Will government programs actually deliver greater equality? Should governmental equality efforts be more about setting guidelines or delivering actual programs? Which forms of equality are most appropriate (certainly education, but also health care, poverty remediation, etc.)? How much should we tax those at the top in order to help those at the bottom? Conservative and liberal administrations have, like sailboats, tacked back and forth on these questions.

Now, however, some Progressives seek to move to a new set of equality questions. Are radical changes needed to our economic system to redistribute power by delivering greater income or wealth equality? Is there, in fact, no real equality until we address these economic questions? Do we need a worldwide change to a much more progressive tax to reduce economic inequality? Is it necessary to not only focus on those at the bottom and how to bring them up but also to take away from those at the top as a principle of equality? Small steps have been taken in this new direction, including new taxes on wealth or on the very top incomes.

Just as historians have debated whether Lyndon Johnson's Great Society moved America from equality of opportunity to equality of outcome, one wonders whether these new ideas would constitute a turning away from equality of opportunity as a long-cherished American goal of the American system. Is equality of opportunity to be replaced by equality of outcome or income? Or are vague notions of equity now the goal?

Even as the debate has widened, it seems that, in the end, it is still about equality of opportunity. But we would argue that equality of opportunity rightly understood is not really a set of government programs or policy prescriptions. Since we understand that complete equality is not possible, the proper understanding of equality of opportunity is as a point of departure and an aspiration, both a starting point and a goal toward which the society is always working. The key question, then, is not whether equality of opportunity is outdated as a goal, but whether we are continuing to make progress toward it. Measuring and discussing progress is the key, not changing the finish line. This is especially so since, as it has been since the Founding, the goal of equality in American terms must also be balanced with individual liberty.

There are reasons to be optimistic about the future of equality of opportunity. For one thing, the American people believe it describes the American dream better than equality of outcome or other formulations of the goal. For another, immigrants by the millions keep coming to America in search of opportunity, so they see something here that perhaps long-settled Americans have lost. Then, too, young people keep looking for new frontiers and opportunities, finding new jobs, new careers, other parts of the country that support their dreams. There is cause for philosophical optimism in that some are deeply committed to equality, others to liberty and opportunity, but the combination—equality of opportunity—is still a middle ground upon which they can gather.

We should acknowledge, however, that there are also reasons for pessimism about the future of equality of opportunity. In this day of hyper-partisanship, when people are dug into their particular points of view, a middle ground is hard to find, much less get to. Those on the left could dig in ever deeper on equality and equity, while those on the right advocate liberty and opportunity. Compromise has become a dirty word. Indeed, young people especially express a loss of faith in American democracy and its economic system of capitalism. In point of fact, with poor civic education, they do not even understand them well.

Whatever happened to equality of opportunity? It is still alive and well, but it needs to be appreciated for what it is, a point of departure and an aspiration, not for what it is not, a set of policies or government programs. Government can and will contribute to pursuing the aspiration, but not to the exclusion of efforts by individuals, nonprofits, and the larger society. The clearest way to kill American equality of opportunity would be to reduce it to a set of government economic and social programs—a possibility if the new New Left has its way. As immigrants teach us, America is still a land of opportunity as well as equality. And as economists in the tradition of Milton Friedman remind us: big government provides huge incentives for us not to be self-reliant. Do the welfare state and participatory socialism, with their focus on equal outcomes, destroy our incentives to work, to save and invest in ourselves, our families, and our communities? Whatever happens, we must not allow this to happen to equality of opportunity.

Notes

1. Ron Haskins and Isabel Sawhill, *Creating an Opportunity Society* (Washington, DC: Brookings Institution Press, 2009), 1–2.

2. Pew Research Center, "2012 American Values Survey," https://www .pewresearch.org/politics/values; State Policy Network, "American Voters' Views on Equality of Opportunity," State Policy Network blog, July 13, 2022, https://spn.org /blog/american-voters-views-on-equality-of-opportunity.

3. "Equality vs. Equity," Kamala Harris vice presidential campaign video, 00:50, Twitter, November 1, 2020, https://twitter.com/kamalaharris/status/132296332199 4289154?lang=en.

4. John E. Roemer, *Equality of Opportunity* (Cambridge, MA: Harvard University Press, 1998), 1–7.

5. Elizabeth M. Smith-Pryor, "Equal Opportunity Is Not Enough. Equality Is in Outcomes," *Star-Tribune* (Minneapolis), July 15, 2020.

6. Robert Cherry, "The Damaging Effects of Shifting from Equal Opportunity to 'Equal Outcomes,'" *The Hill*, December 11, 2020.

7. Cherry.

8. Milton Friedman and Rose Friedman, *Free to Choose: A Personal Statement* (New York: Harcourt Brace Jovanovich, 1980), 136.

9. Tunku Varadarajan, "How Equality Lost to Equity," *Wall Street Journal*, February 12, 2021.

10. See Martha Minow, "Equality vs. Equity," *American Journal of Law and Equality* 1 (2021): 167–93.

11. Thomas Piketty, *Capital in the Twenty-First Century* (Cambridge, MA: Belknap Press, 2014); Thomas Piketty, *Capital and Ideology* (Cambridge, MA: Belknap Press, 2020); Thomas Piketty, *A Brief History of Equality* (Cambridge, MA: Belknap Press, 2022).

12. Piketty, *Capital and Ideology*, 471–73.

13. Piketty, 508–9.

14. Piketty, 515.

15. Piketty, 517–18.

16. Piketty, 512.

17. Piketty, 41, 1036.

18. Piketty, *Brief History*, 2, 17.

19. Piketty, 22.

20. Piketty, 26.

21. Piketty, 42, 46.

22. Piketty, 150.

23. Piketty, 155.

24. Bernie Sanders, "Tax on Extreme Wealth," Friends of Bernie Sanders (website), accessed October 20, 2022, https://berniesanders.com/issues/tax-extreme-wealth.

25. Sanders.

26. Zolan Kanno-Youngs, "Biden to Include Minimum Tax on Billionaires in Budget Proposal," *New York Times*, March 28, 2022.

27. Stacey Rutland, "After Roe, Families Need Universal Basic Income More Than Ever," *Time*, July 13, 2022.

28. Jason Lalljee, "33 Basic and Guaranteed Income Programs Where Cities and States Give Direct Payments to Residents, No Strings Attached," *Business Insider*, December 16, 2021.

29. "Our Key Findings," Stockton Economic Empowerment Demonstration website, accessed November 11, 2022, https://www.stocktondemonstration.org.

30. Ran Abramitzky and Leah Boustan, *Streets of Gold: America's Untold Story of Immigrant Success* (New York: Hachette Book Group, 2022).

31. Peter Coy, "Why So Many Children of Immigrants Rise to the Top," *New York Times*, July 10, 2022.

32. Mark Hugo Lopez and Mohamad Moslimani, "Latinos See US as Better Than Place of Family's Ancestry for Opportunity, Raising Kids, Health Care Access," Pew Research Center Report, January 20, 2022.

33. Raj Chetty, "Improving Equality of Opportunity: New Insights from Big Data," *Contemporary Economic Policy* 39, no. 1 (January 2021): 7–41.

34. Chetty, 39.

35. Scott Winship, *Economic Mobility in America: A State of the Art Primer*, Archbridge Institute, November 2021.

36. Michael Lachanski, "Three Myths about US Economic Inequality and Social Mobility," Niskanen Center, April 6, 2022.

37. Michael Itzkowitz, "Out with the Old, In with the New: Rating Higher Ed by Economic Mobility," Third Way Report, January 27, 2022.

38. Joseph E. Stiglitz, "Equal Opportunity, Our National Myth," *New York Times*, February 16, 2013.

39. William F. Meehan III, "John Hennessy: The Leader as Principled Pragmatist Considers the Five Fates," Forbes.com, October 11, 2019.

40. See, e.g., Henry Braun, "The Dynamics of Opportunity in America: A Working Framework," in *The Dynamics of Opportunity in America*, eds. Irwin Kirsch and Henry Braun (New York: Springer, 2016), 160.

41. See, e.g., Bruno V. Manno, "A Better Way to Promote Equality of Opportunity through Education," *Merion West*, March 28, 2022.

42. Rachel Fishman, Ernest Ezeugo, and Sophie Nguyen, "Americans Believe Education after High School Creates Opportunities," *Varying Degrees 2018: New America's Annual Survey on Higher Education*, New America, last updated May 21, 2018.

ABOUT THE AUTHORS

David Davenport and **Gordon Lloyd** are the coauthors of three previous books: *The New Deal and Modern American Conservatism: A Defining Rivalry* (2013), *Rugged Individualism: Dead Or Alive?* (2017), and *How Public Policy Became War* (2019).

David Davenport is a research fellow at the Hoover Institution, where he has also served as counselor to the director and director of Washington, DC, programs. He is also a senior fellow at the Ashbrook Center. He previously served as president of Pepperdine University, where he was a professor of public policy and law. He has been a regular columnist for the *Washington Examiner*, *Forbes.com*, the *San Francisco Chronicle*, and the Scripps Howard News Service.

Gordon Lloyd is a senior fellow at the Ashbrook Center and the Dockson Professor Emeritus of Public Policy at Pepperdine University. He is coauthor of three books on the American Founding and is editor of James Madison's *Debates in the Federal Convention of 1787*. He is also the creator of several websites on the Founding, the Constitution, and the Bill of Rights.

INDEX

Nixon, Richard
 Philadelphia Plan, 70
 support and expansion of Great Society
  initiatives, 55, 69–70
 TV debate with Kennedy, 26

Obama, Barack, 97, 106
"opportunity society," 77–78, 83–84, 97, 107
"opportunity theory" approach, 54
Orenstein, Norman J., 64
Other America, The (Harrington), 61–62,
 64, 72

patrimonial capitalism, 98
People's History of the United States, A
 (Zinn), 107
Pew Research Center
 equality of opportunity principle, 91
 immigration and opportunities, 105
Philadelphia Plan, 70
Piketty, Thomas, 98–100, 104
Poor Ye Need Not Have With You, The
 (Levine), 63
poverty
 relieving poverty vs. creating opportunity,
  62–63
 War on Poverty, 49–50, 61–63, 72
Progressive era
 Coolidge's pushback against big
  government, 21
 Herbert Croly, 13–14
 "frontier thesis," 12–13
 Harding's pushback against big
  government, 20–21
 Hoover's pushback against big
  government, 21
 overview, 12–14
 Theodore Roosevelt, 14–15
 Woodrow Wilson, 15–20
Promise of American Life, The (Croly), 13

Rauchway, Eric, 42
Reagan, Ronald, 108
 approach to problems of Black
  Americans, 82–83
 CPAC speech of 1974, 80–82

debate with George Bush in 1980, 82
equality plans, 84–87
on failure of war on poverty, 72
Family Support Act of 1988, 86
Franklin Roosevelt vs., 82
government deregulation, 80–81
Low-Income Opportunity Improvement
 Act of 1987, 85
Medicare Catastrophic Coverage Act of
 1988, 87
"Noble vision" speech, 83–84
Notre Dame speech, 78–79
"opportunity society," 77–78, 83–84, 107
Reaganomics, 81
"supply-side economics," 80
support of New Deal, 78–79
tax policy, 79–80
"A Time for Choosing" speech, 65–66,
 74–77
view of role of government in equality of
 opportunity, 97
"Remember the Ladies" letter (Abigail
 Adams), 10
republican form of government
 Founding era, 8–9
 Madison's belief in, 6–7
Revolution (Anderson), 71
Road to Serfdom (Hayek), 73
Roosevelt, Franklin. *See also* New Deal
 Commonwealth Club speech, 1–2, 12,
  25–26, 28–30, 31, 32, 35
 first hundred days, 40
 "the forgotten man" concept, 26, 32,
  36–37
 "four freedoms speech," 42
 Hoover-Roosevelt debates, 26–28
 Lyndon Johnson as disciple of, 47
 New Deal, 4
 "re-appraisal of values," 30, 31
 Ronald Reagan vs., 82
 second inaugural address, 42
 State of the Union speech, 1944, 42
 view of role of government in equality of
  opportunity, 96
Roosevelt, Theodore, 14–16, 43
rugged individualism, 1, 33–35